For every
who wants

Are you still furious at your ex-husband? Resentful when he spends money on a new girl friend? Outraged when he misses an alimony or child care payment? Do you spend endless hours reliving old arguments and rehearsing new ones? Your life is still filled with rage. And it's not your ex-husband (or ex-lover) who's hurt by your anger—it's you.

HOW TO FORGIVE YOUR EX-HUSBAND (AND GET ON WITH YOUR LIFE) is *not* about being "a nice person." It's a step-by-step guide to dealing with the stormy feelings that can overwhelm you, making peace with the past, and freeing your time, your energies, and your emotions *away* from thoughts of "him," and toward building a happy future for *you*.

Written by two women who have lived through the experience themselves, and illustrated with case histories, this insightful book shows what happens in many marriages and through many exercises and quizzes, helps you understand and successfully resolve what happened in yours.

HOW TO
Forgive
YOUR
EX-HUSBAND
(and Get On With) Your Life

Marcia Hootman and Patt Perkins

WARNER BOOKS

A Warner Communications Company

WARNER BOOKS EDITION

This Warner Books Edition is published by arrangement with
Doubleday & Company, Inc.

Warner Books, Inc.
666 Fifth Avenue
New York, N.Y. 10103

A Warner Communications Company

Printed in the United States of America

First Warner Books Printing: January, 1985

10 9 8 7 6 5 4 3 2 1

To all those willing to do whatever it takes
to clean up the wreckage of the past.

Patt and Marcia

Preface

There are very few of us who, at the precise moment of separation, don't have some very strong feelings about what could have been instead of what actually was. It could be a reflection on the past—if he had only been a better husband or lover; if I had been a better wife; if I had tried a little harder, it could have worked.

We worry about our future, the future of our children and trading what we know for what we don't know. "Do I have the ability to support myself financially?" "Can I be effective as a single parent?" "How can I, after living with this man on an intense, intimate level, now adjust to a detached social and business relationship?" "Do I want to go back to the dating game?"

Is the final decree really final, or is it just the beginning of a different set of challenges? The momentary exhilaration of freedom may have turned into feelings of aloneness, confusion and self-doubt.

Since the release of this book, reactions to the the title have been surprising. On our promotional van we have signs on each side with reproductions of the cover of the book. Wherever we go heads turn, followed by a thumbs-up, laughter or a negative shrug. Everyone who reads the title has some kind of opinion about it, which indicates to us the importance of this subject.

Some men say, "Why isn't it *How to Forgive Your Ex-Wife?* We always get the blame." In a way, the book is not about ex-husbands, but ex-anythings. This is *not* an antimale book, nor does it presuppose that the breakup was his fault. On the contrary, we have taken a fresh, new look at the man's point of view.

Women who say, "Why should I forgive him?" are assuming that "to forgive" means to let the other guy off the hook, allow him to be right or give in to him. However, forgiveness *never* has anything to do with the other person. It is simply *a way of getting over the past and insuring that we won't create the same situation again.*

Others who have strong feelings about the subject are young people who are concerned about their mothers who complain to them, fathers whose daughters are going through a bitter divorce, men who send the book to their ex-wives because of a need to clear up the past and current wives who understand how their marriage is affected by resentment from a previous marriage.

After a television show in Kansas City, a young woman called the studio to talk to us off the air. "After reading your book," she said, "particularly the chapter on how we affect our children's lives with our resentment, I decided to stop telling my three-year-old son what a bad man his daddy is." A business woman in Pittsburgh told us about the impact the book had on her life. She had only spoken to her ex-husband in a rude manner for the past five years. On completing the exercises in the book, she made an important decision. She phoned her ex-husband and said, "Why don't we talk on a more human level?" He was relieved and agreed with her immediately. She finally was able to free herself from the agitation of the past. A couple in San Francisco, married for five years, realized divorce was imminent. On a counselor's advice they took the time to read the book together. Their letter to us read, "Thank you for your message. We learned that we didn't have to damage each other while going through this discomfort." Thousands of people who have followed the guidelines we have set down in this book found that they could let go of resentment that was crippling their emotional lives and affecting the lives of those around them.

Just what is resentment? Where does it

come from? Webster defines it as "a feeling of bitter hurt or indignation from a sense of being injured or offended." The central theme of this book is that stifled anger turns into resentment that not only affects your physical and mental well-being, but also *predetermines new relationships*.

Resentment is negative feelings held in the present, for something that happened in the past. What happened yesterday may no longer apply to your life today. The person that you feel created that emotion in you may not be the same person anymore, nor are you the same. Why is it we can accept growth in ourselves, yet close our minds to the possibility of change in others?

Resentment keeps us under the control of whoever or whatever we resent. Resentment locks us into a sequence of act and response, anger and revenge. Each time we think of the person we feel has wronged us, we react in some negative way that is harmful to our well-being. The only way out of resentment is through forgiveness, through releasing the past. To forgive is *to cease to feel resentment against an offender.*

By the time you finish this book, you will learn why forgiveness begins with forgiving yourself and why it is necessary for the quality of your own life. The methods we have used to overcome our anger and resentment have been used by thousands of other women who have learned to live more comfortable lives. We have written this book for those who are still carrying the burden.

Am I, Marcia Hootman, anxiety-driven and domineering?

For seventeen years I thought my ex-husband was the source of my unhappiness; before that I was convinced it was my parents and my childhood environment. The first time I heard anyone tell me I could *choose* to be happy, that *I* was the one controlling my circumstances, I thought she was crazy. But I listened and read all I could. I also did what was suggested. Through perceiving my life in a new way, I soon learned forgiveness was the way out for me. The energy I retrieved from releasing all that held-in resentment I put into moving on with my life. That infusion of energy allowed me to run a successful corporation, further develop my creative talents in music and writing and live an easier, more joyful life.

"Patt Perkins an alcoholic? You must be kidding." There is no kidding about it. At age forty-four, reeling from the breakup of a twenty-seven-year marriage, I began putting my life back together. My lesson in forgiveness was to forgive myself for my past behavior. I also carried guilt feelings about leaving my alcoholic husband while at the same time resenting his way of life. Five years after the divorce, years spent in education and personal growth, the initial feelings came up again, when his alcoholism took his life. It was only by using the principles set forth in this book that I was able to go beyond my alcoholism, my divorce and my ex-husband's death, to an inner peace I had never known before.

The loss of a mate, either through divorce, death or other separation, can bring about the same kinds of feelings and challenges. Sometimes the divorce document or death certificate sets up the beginning of a resentment that can destroy the quality of life for years. Such phrases as "He died on me" or "He left me" are good indications that we are still holding resentment.

In today's lifestyle, couples living together without being married are commonplace. Their situation has created a whole host of new problems. Whether married or unmarried, the pain of a breakup is the same; however, without legal rights to pensions, life insurance or alimony, the unmarried woman is left with very little recourse. Palimony suits are long, expensive and exhausting. The average woman doesn't have the time or money to pursue such an issue. Nor does the unmarried woman get a sympathetic ear from society. Although living together may set well with the individuals involved, there still seems to be moral judgment from certain segments of every community. In many ways a breakup leaves an unmarried woman feeling more devastated, more helpless and more victimized than her divorced counterpart.

Sadness and loss are universal. Pain doesn't recognize the existence of a marriage document. This book is dedicated to bringing you out of the hurts of the past and into the infinite possibilities of the future.

Both of our journeys took six years, but that time span is not a requirement for changing your life. Had we been exposed earlier to the specific kind of thinking and techniques spelled out for you here, it may have taken less time.

Practical exercises included at the end of each chapter will easily lead you through a day-by-day process. Beginning with recognition you will get a clear picture of the patterns you set up. The response portion is a self-questioning exercise that may turn up some surprising answers for you. Using the reinforcement techniques, you will be provided with daily reminders of what you've learned.

The best place to practice these is the place most comfortable for *you*, where there won't be outside interference. We find that some deep-breathing exercises prior to beginning these techniques is also beneficial. For example, try the following. Breathing through your nose, fill your lungs slowly to a count of four. Open your mouth and slowly exhale. Repeat three times. From the reinforcement portion, choose whichever statement means the most to you. Write it on a small card and place it somewhere in your house, office or car where you will notice it often. You will find yourself subvocalizing it automatically each time you look at it. Don't feel pressured to do every exercise. Take only what seems to fit you and leave the rest. This can be a lifetime process, because what doesn't fit you now may serve you later.

Your willingness to read this book is your first step in moving along on a wonderful journey where you can receive benefits that are beyond what you now imagine. Abundance, harmony and well-being can be yours when you make the decision to accept them. This decision can take you to greater freedom than you have been able to experience up to this time—freedom from the bondage of your troubled thoughts. It is possible for your perception to expand to a point where you will have peace of mind and a sense of joy you have not felt in years.

Be assured that there are others just like you, women suffering with the same doubts and fears. You may find them in your close circle of friends or in outside support groups. You are not alone. All you need do is ask.

Marcia Hootman
Patt Perkins
La Jolla, California
February 1984

Contents

How much does a grudge weigh?

All that we put into the lives of others comes into our own.

Anonymous

She slammed the phone down. All the old feelings of rage and resentment came back. "Well, he's done it to me again!"

Forgive whom? It's easy to tell our friends they need to forgive someone, but what about us? We're different. The wrong we feel has been done us always seems greater than what any other person on this earth has ever experienced. We get the feeling "I'm alone," "I'm different." We feel that our story is unique, and, surely, the experience greater than anyone else's. Viktor Frankl, in *Man's Search for Meaning*,[1] explains it by saying that pain is like the gas in a hot-air balloon. No matter how

---

[1] Viktor E. Frankl, *Man's Search for Meaning: An Introduction to Logotherapy* (New York: Simon & Schuster, 1963).

large the balloon is, the substance fills it completely.

No matter the size of our pain, anger or resentment—no matter how deep the hurt or the turmoil in our lives—it totally fills our being. If I have a toothache, I may consider *that* the ultimate pain at the moment. You may say to me, "But I just lost my son." Yet we both experience our individual pain and suffering as total, overwhelming. We become egocentric in our own minds, thinking we are the center of the universe, and, as such, demand all the attention we can get. Through our efforts to keep that attention focused on us we keep telling our "soap opera" stories of how bad it was and how angry we are at "him."

Sometimes we deny our resentment, although it may be that we just buried it. Many times we have thought, "Oh, no, I have no resentment against anyone." We become righteous, martyrlike, saying, "I'm wonderful; I'm a good person, above that sort of unworthy feeling."

But if we pay attention to our words and our physical sensations when we speak of a particular person or incident in our past, we may discover some lingering resentment.

Barbara recalls the year after separation from her husband, a year filled with the fear of losing custody of her son:

"When the movie *Kramer vs. Kramer* came out and friends would invite me to go see it, my immediate reaction was 'I don't want to see that movie; I lived it!' I was still hanging on to some of the resentment I felt while going through the custody battle for my oldest son. In telling my 'soap opera' I would say, 'He insisted on having Mike in court. Do you know he had a marshal subpeona that kid? Woke him up at six one morning.' In fact, we were both up every morning at five-thirty anyway, but making it sound like a hardship to be awakened was another way I could make my ex-husband wrong."

Although Barbara was ultimately awarded custody of her son, she knew she still had some forgiving to do when she paid attention to her feelings and choice of words in retelling her story.

Janet married her childhood sweetheart. When she was in her early twenties, her husband left her with a young daughter to support. In spite of her financial and personal burden, Janet learned how to appreciate the gifts in her life.

Janet's ex-husband promised to send his daughter a present. She went to the mailbox every day for over a month, expecting a gift, but never finding it. He didn't send it. The emotion Janet felt was sadness; the tears welled up in her eyes when she saw little Jeannie coming back empty-handed from the mailbox. She recalls the angry thought, "How dare he break a promise to a child." The tightness in Janet's throat and the rigidity of her body were only the immediate physical manifestations of her resentment. Mentally she felt immobilized because she simply couldn't remove that pain.

Is there anyone in your life that can evoke those feelings—those little hurts? How do you feel when you hear your ex-husband is doing well without you in his career or his love life, or that he weighs ten pounds less than he did when you were married? How do you feel when your kids tell you how happy they are to see him? When you hear about him buying that beautiful new home overlooking the ocean—with his new wife—do you get any twinges of envy? Do you wonder why he treats *her* children so well? Have you seen that "rock" she is wearing on her finger? Comedienne Joan Rivers says you can always tell a first wife from a second by the size of the ring. Do you wonder how he can afford all the things he never wanted to buy for you?

Joyce, in her late thirties, lived in an affluent suburban community, with her three teenage children. Since her divorce ten years ago, she has gone back to court three times, in an attempt to collect unpaid child support.

The first time Joyce went into court to

retrieve unpaid child support, her biggest frustration was that her ex-husband could afford to send his high-paid attorney to represent him at the hearing, when she had no money to do so. "How can he afford to pay a lawyer, when he can't afford to support his own flesh and blood?" she asked.

Here are some of the kinds of statements we hear all the time:

"He's got money to take her out, but none to give his kids."

"You should see the expensive new outfit he was wearing."

"How can he afford that twenty-five-dollar haircut?"

"So he bought a new ten-speed bike. Why is he so active now? I couldn't get him away from the football games on TV."

"Why is he going to all those fancy places he would never take me?"

"I heard he was downtown shopping. He never went shopping with me!"

"What in the world would a twenty-year-old want with him?"

If you can hear yourself saying any of the above—or a similar variation—you may be holding on to something from the past, which could be controlling your present relationships and your life in general. "Your attention is the same as your power. If your attention is locked up in the past, you don't have the power to change your life now."[2] You can now decide whether or not to use your power negatively, or to create a more positive life.

Why is it necessary to let resentment go? Studies by Dr. Elisabeth Kubler-Ross[3] show the most common aspect of the chronically ill is unfinished business from the past. Forgiving someone has nothing to do with being a good person. Nor does it have anything to do with the other person—letting him off the hook. Many women have told us they were not *ready* to forgive their ex-husbands, as if that resentment they held so tenaciously could affect him.

Forgiveness is entirely selfish. "When a person comes into your life, he becomes a piece of your mind. If you later condemn him, it's as if you are kicking a piece of your mind, making it sore."[4] Do you want to keep kicking yourself? Releasing resentment is necessary and essential for your own well-being. Holding on to animosity is like taking small doses of poison. Little by little you become sicker and sicker. It begins to destroy your physical and mental well-being.

[2] Dr. Robert Lorenz, *L.A. Weekly*, August 13–19, 1982.

[3] Elisabeth Kubler-Ross has done extensive work with terminally ill people and their families. Her writings include *On Death and Dying* (New York: Macmillan Co., 1970).

[4] Hugh Prather, lecturer and author of *Notes to Myself* (Moab, Utah: Real People Press, 1970). Quoted from a talk given September 4, 1982, San Diego, California.

Unvented anger traditionally turns itself into depression. Dr. Theodore Rubin describes depression as an adult temper tantrum. "It represents anger at one's self directly and anger at other people, displaced and directed at one's self. It is one of the most prevalent forms of anger directed at one's self."[5] If you cannot get your anger or resentment out, thereby releasing it, it must turn inward, get stuffed down, suppressed into some other level of your consciousness where it stays like a festering open wound. If that wound isn't cleaned out, it can turn into an infection: resentment.

Suppression has been called "the emotional plague of man" by Dr. Wilhelm Reich. "The goal of suppression is to diminish the life force."[6] As soon as you diminish your life force, Eros, you make way for Thanatos, the death force or illness, to come in. Physically, suppresssed anger or resentment can be manifested as a lack of energy or chronic illnesses, particularly those diseases that have as symptoms some type of inflexibility, constriction or holding in. Arthritis, constipation and lower back pain are some of the more obvious.

---

[5] Dr. Theodore Isaac Rubin, *Reconciliations—Inner Peace in an Age of Anxiety* (New York: The Viking Press, 1980).

[6] Wilhelm Reich, noted psychotherapist.

Think of a time when you were angry and try to recall how your body felt. You probably held your breath and were so mad you "couldn't see straight." If you are anything like me, your heart started pounding furiously, your blood pressure rose and you felt you wanted to inflict bodily harm.

According to Ken Wilber's work,[7] if you feel like striking out or yelling and do neither, you are physically suppressing some muscle action. You are using some muscles in your body to pull back the other muscles; half of your muscles are trying to get rid of the hostility, the other half of them are straining to prevent it. Neither set of muscles wins out, but the anger and tension bury themselves inside your body. What do you think that stalemate might do to your body?

Other less critical symptoms of withheld resentment or anger may be interrupted sleep patterns. Sometimes you awaken because you can't stop playing those "old tapes" about what everyone did to you, or what you think they did to you. They continue to run through your brain.

If we all could learn the lesson of forgive-

---

[7] Ken Wilber is regarded as the foremost writer on transpersonal psychology. His works include *No Boundary, Eastern and Western Approaches to Personal Growth* (Boulder, Colorado: Shambhala Publications, Inc., 1979) and *Up from Eden, a Transpersonal View of Human Evolution* (Garden City, N.Y.: Anchor Press/Doubleday, 1981).

ness and acceptance, how long would sleeping pill companies stay in business? Interrupted sleep alone, night after night, can sap our energy. If our sleep is artificially induced, chances are we will wake up after eight or ten hours of deep sleep and not feel rested at all.

You can usually tell when you have unfinished business with someone. You may overindulge in food, alcohol or sleep. If it is sleep you choose, you will somehow convince yourself that your problem will be gone when you wake up. The trouble is that when you regain consciousness you know it hasn't disappeared. Often you will feel more tired than when you went to sleep. If you are having problems with not enough (or too much) sleep, you may want to take a look at what's really going on. If your one-martini lunches are turning into four-martini marathons, ask yourself why you are trying to dull your senses so much. If you are constantly bingeing on food, explore why you can never be satisfied.

You can choose fatigue or energy, illness or health. But physical well-being is only one reason for you to forgive. The quality of your life, from this moment on, depends on it.

Please don't play it again, Sam

Negativity cannot create, it can only repeat.
Anonymous

When you are convinced that someone hurt you in the past, you may fear that another person will do the same thing in the future. You start to think people are not trustworthy and become fearful of making any new commitments. "Every time I really fall in love, I get hurt." This kind of thinking will prevent you from creating healthy relationships despite the opportunities—and willingness on your part.

If you enter a new relationship with any judgments held over from the last one, you will re-create the former one again and again. "Problems keep coming up because they [keep] giving you an opportunity to handle them in a new way, in order to move on."[1]

[1] John Niendorff, *Listen to the Light* (Los Angeles: Science of Mind Publications, 1980).

Laura, a bright, sensitive woman in her middle thirties, carried with her from childhood feelings of inadequacy, resentment for her parents and a sense of isolation. These emotions dictated her behavior for many years after her divorce. Three months after separation, she jumped into another long-term relationship.

"Everyone told me I would, but I said, 'No, not I.' This was the real thing. Charles was different. I was swept away into another fairy tale with Prince Charming coming to the rescue again. But this time I was all together, or so I assumed. I took the focus off myself, just as I had done in my marriage, and put all my energies into cementing a close relationship.

"To be with Charles, I spent weekends doing what he wanted to, because I felt lost when he wasn't around. I gave up everything I liked to do. I was emotionally dependent on him, just as I had been with my husband. Away from Charles I felt incomplete. I needed to have him around, even though I never felt loved when I was with him. As different as I thought Charles was from my husband, I found the most critical parallel.

"Both Charles and my ex-husband were people who liked to be alone. I had not yet handled my own aloneness, so that devastated me. They were more comfortable reading a good book than socializing. They craved privacy, and preferred to be out drinking with the boys than being with me. After two years, I gave Charles an ultimatum. I know now that ultimatums are the kiss of death to any relationship. We were to move in together, or it was all over. Obviously, he couldn't meet my demands, so I simply cut off the relationship—just as I had done in my marriage. At that time, I realized I had put myself back in the same dependent position I had been in before I got my divorce and I didn't want to stop my growth again. That was only part of it. The biggest excuse was that just like my ex-husband, Charles wouldn't shape up either.

"Surely *I* had no problems. I thought he was unreasonable and stubborn. Why would he pass up a chance to live with me? Thank God he did. I will be eternally grateful for everyone in my life just like Charles who said 'No' to me so I could say 'Yes' to myself. In retrospect I saw how I created the same type of relationship I had given up before. And if I didn't change something, I would do it again. What was controlling me was the 'old tape,' the old voice, 'If you love me, why do you keep leaving me alone?'"

"Personal unfinished business cannot be resolved by another," says Dr. Paul Brenner.[2] If

---

[2] Dr. Paul Brenner, *Life Is a Shared Creation* (Marina del Rey, California: DeVorss, Publishers, 1981).

you are holding any resentment toward any-one—your mother or father, friend, ex-boss, ex-mate, you are stuck. You will find another person who treats you the same way, and ultimately your relationship is destined to be a repeat of your last one. Because we always go back to what is familiar, we keep trying to create—with each new person—the interpersonal conflicts of early childhood.

Three steps are necessary to stop that some-times vicious circle of love, intimacy, disappointment and resentment:

1) *Complete the relationship*.

Tell the other person everything you have not been willing to say before. Tell the truth about your feelings, coming from a stance of "I," not "you"—own up to your part in the problem. In place of saying "You always yell at me," it's "When you get angry, I feel scared." Rather than "You're continually breaking your promises," "When you don't keep your promises, I feel hurt."

2) *Release the other person*.

Give up your attachment to the form of the relationship. This kind of honesty can convert a torrid love affair into a lifelong friendship. But be ready to accept that the other person may not respond at all.

3) *Re-context all your relationships.*

Be honest from the start about your expectations, giving the other person the freedom to be and do what he wishes to, and keep the lines of communication clear—that is, handle each little minor irritation as it comes up, not later, blown out of proportion and out of context.

And what of self-worth? Maybe we really think we are not worth the love and appreciation we say we want. Maybe all those things he supposedly did to us were well deserved. Is there a sneaking suspicion that he was right all along?

Amanda, a well-educated businesswoman in her early thirties, was married at age seventeen. She was a product of criticizing parents and married a man who also seemed to find fault in everything she did. Years later, shortly after her divorce, Amanda tried to cover up her feelings of inadequacy by conforming to the same negative pattern.

"I thought that as long as I had someone to put down, I could feel better about me. But somewhere deep inside my soul, a tiny voice told me I wasn't okay. Through two long years of searching for answers, I came to realize that the only person I really needed to forgive was myself, for allowing the hurt to happen. I also came to the awareness that everything in my life that has occurred so far was for a specific purpose. If I look back at what seemed disasters at the time, I realize what opportunities they actually were. Had I not been fired from that secretarial job, I may have been doing that all my life. I quit teaching because, in retrospect, I couldn't deal with working at the same school where my ex-husband worked. If I hadn't quit teaching, I would never have gone into real estate and been able to enjoy the life I now have. I can look back and see where each time I thought I would be devastated for life, the result was a blessing for me."

Amanda's search paid off for her. As soon as she gave up blaming others for doing it to her, she could move on. She discovered that whenever one door closes, another one opens. What you consider disasters in your life may also be *your* blessings in disguise.

Janet, a divorced single parent, was repeatedly turned down for jobs. When she applied to be a chicken plucker, they refused to hire her because she had a young infant at home. Later, she tried desperately to pass a typing test three times, but could never qualify. The jobs she was able to get carried her through college. Upon graduation she was hired by a small, growing company. A management shake-up led her to a decision to leave.

With two men who also left, Janet decided to start her own company. Two years later the firm was still struggling, and Janet's partners quit. What could have been viewed as another disappointment in her life Janet took as an opportunity. From that first shaky start, Janet built her company into a multimillion-dollar enterprise.

GROW, Giving and Receiving Organization for Women, is a large networking group headquartered in San Diego, California. The women who attend these weekly meetings run from judges and physicians to secretaries and homemakers. Each time a member announces that she has either been terminated or quit her job, the entire group applauds enthusiastically. These bright, positive women, based upon their own experience, can relate to the exhilaration and fear that accompany such a shift. "Now a new adventure begins," one group member remarked. "You can build your inner strength and have an opportunity to grow."

It could be that the personal disappointments you have gone through are only indications that there is something better waiting for you. If you keep thinking about the past, you cannot move on to that something better.

Just how much time do you spend thinking about the past instead of the present? And how many hours have you spent discussing "him" with your friends and relatives? Think of what you could be doing more productively with your time to nurture yourself and plan for your own future, if you will let go of the past. How much better off could you be by working on that one person you have control over in life—you?

If you are spending hours thinking about how it was, and about your ex-mate, you are giving him control over your life and your happiness. By thinking about him you are reminding yourself that he was the only source of your good, and without him (or another man) you can do nothing. You need to bring yourself out of these thoughts in order to make positive decisions about your life.

Mrs. Jones, age fifty, newly divorced, continues to drive a car that breaks down. She knows she needs to buy another one, but does not want to go through the motions. "My ex-husband always picked out our cars. I don't know which one to buy. What if I get taken?" Her unwillingness to make her own decisions allows her to delay taking some kind of positive action in her life. Mrs. Jones can keep driving the "old clunker," resent her husband for not being there to assist her in the decision, and stay stuck in the syndrome of "I should but I don't know how. If he hadn't left me, this wouldn't be happening."

Mrs. Jones forgot that car-buying was always a joint decision. He had never gone out and brought a car back without first asking for her opinion.

In fact, she was always involved in car-buying. Even now, on some level, she knows she has a choice. She can keep driving the old car and blame her ex-husband, or buy a new one. In order to buy a new car, she can figure out what she requires of an automobile. Is mileage important? Does she need a sedan or a coupe? Would a brand-new or used car be better? She can then find out, through various consumer guides and other reputable sources, which make of car would suit her. A chat with her banker would provide her with financing information.

Mrs. Jones refuses to take these simple steps. She would rather hang on to her resentment than take any responsibility for her own decisions. Her friends reinforce her problem by sympathizing and listening interminably.

Are you allowing others to support and nurture your resentment by seeking their advice and encouragement? (Mrs. Jones was.)

"I found that most of my friends were willing to listen to my story and agree with me. Not only would they agree, they would be tremendously sympathetic to my plight, which only served to keep me more entrenched in what I believed. I experienced a sort of 'choosing up sides' after my divorce. The friends my husband and I had during our marriage seemed to be compelled to be for or against one of us." Those on Mrs. Jones's side supported and nurtured her resentment. It won't be until after she stops getting validation for her feelings, for what she says, that she can realistically see her one-sided perception of things, her desire to have someone else to blame for her lot in life. For now Mrs. Jones prefers to blame her ex-husband for the way her life is working; she can be right *and* play victim.

When is it time to give up resentment? It may be when you realize your life is not moving in a positive direction. Dr. Harold Bloomfield[3] says that peace is healing past resentments. You may not associate certain challenges in your life with hidden resentments; however, they could be what is holding you back from joy, prosperity, success and general good feelings. If you can't really define why your life isn't exactly the way you want it to be, it may be you are ready to deal with

---

[3] Dr. Harold Bloomfield is a nationally known psychiatrist, author and lecturer. His books include *How to Survive the Loss of a Love*, Melba Colgrove, Ph. D., Harold Bloomfield and Peter McWilliams (New York: Bantam Books, 1976) and *Making Peace with Your Parents* (New York: Random House, 1983).

forgiveness on all levels. Are you at peace with yourself?

"Won't I ever learn?" "I did it again." "Why do I keep doing that?"

These unanswered questions show us how we keep beating ourselves up mentally for not being all we can be. We often begin by making other people the villains. "If he hadn't done this to me, I wouldn't feel this way."

Instead of admitting "I did it, now how can I resolve it or learn from it?" we sometimes try to put the guilt on others.

Johnny told his mother he accidentally tracked mud onto the kitchen floor. Mom, just having waxed it, spanked him. The next time Johnny forgot to wipe his feet, he blamed his little brother. Having been punished in the past, we get the idea we should never admit to a mistake.

We are, in fact, creatures born to make mistakes. That is the only way in which we learn. There is nothing wrong with making an error in judgment. Research is based on eliminating all the mistakes first to get to the solution. If you can get them all out of the way, you will arrive at the answer. Jet planes are off course almost ninety percent of the time. The crew monitors the instruments and makes corrections accordingly. They still arrive at their planned destination.

Betty and Don's twenty-year marriage was

set up like a 1960s situation comedy. He was a young U.S. Army officer whose role was bread-winner and decision maker. In return Betty was to be a loving wife and mother of their three children. When their youngest son moved into his teens, Betty longed for a new role. She started a part-time job and a few months later realized that the new world she found became more precious to her than her marital role. She had a new identity as Betty, not merely Don's wife or Joe's mother. Her yearnings for a less restrictive life, yet her unwillingness to struggle with Don to have it, led her to seek a divorce.

Don was unwilling to move out of the house. He also threatened her with a long custody battle if she tried to take the children. Not wanting to put the children through the pain, Betty agreed to find an apartment.

She never thought the mother/child relationship would change. Yet she sensed that her children were angry at her for leaving. Don reinforced their anger by letting them know he had wanted to do anything to keep the family together, but "*She* left us."

Although the children never voiced their anger, Betty could feel it. At first she felt that her children were abandoning her, emotionally. From there she took on the guilt that perhaps she had abandoned them.

"The guilt drove me into a deep depression.

All the other guilts I felt from my whole life came tumbling in. I was in it so deep, I knew my choice was either to die or let go of the guilt. I chose life over death because I didn't want to hurt them any more than I had already done."

Through professional help, Betty remembered her decision to leave was to avoid further pain, not to cause it. She began to understand that she deserved her own life and knew she couldn't move in a positive direction if she was still hanging on to the past. She knew that as long as she beat herself up with self-recrimination, she would convince herself that she was not worthy. Her feelings of unworthiness would keep her from doing what she wanted to do. She had to begin by forgiving herself.

"How do I start forgiving?" First recognize that you have someone to forgive or accept by becoming aware that you are holding on to resentment. Then be willing to take action.

Jesus advised forgiving seventy times seven (Matthew 18:22). You can begin by writing "I forgive myself" (my mother, Joe, etc.) seventy times, for seven days. There is no magic in the number of times you write it. The magic comes because each time you write it, you also subvocalize it. If, after 400 times there are still little twinges of resentment over that particular person, do it some more. It's like cleaning out a plastic soap bottle. Even after washing it a long time, little remnants of soap bubbles keep surfacing. You must keep cleansing it with clear water until *all* the bubbles disappear.

To further overcome those feelings, explore carefully all the little resentments in your life. Specifically identify who and how many people you have these feelings for. How many friends or relatives would you hesitate telling you loved them? What would a card have to express to wish your ex-husband a happy birthday? What would tell it the way you really feel it? Continue to ask yourself these questions and don't be surprised if your answers change each day.

After several years of study and reading about accepting others and their contribution to our lives and after a lot of introspection and questioning about her life, Gail knew she needed to give up her primary resentment—the unexpressed anger toward her mother. Gail recalls the process:

"At Christmas time three years ago, Mom came to visit me. It was then that I finally understood that she had always done the very best she could, and after all, I didn't grow up emotionally or physically damaged. The person I grew into had a great deal to do with her. I began by writing her a short note. It went something like 'I'm glad you are my mother. I love you.' I wasn't sure I meant it, but it seemed to be good practice and I knew I was ready to get rid of those old feelings that were keeping me from the quality of life I desired. From that first step I developed a deep understanding of my relationship with my mother, who she really is, who I am and what part we have had and continue to have in each other's lives. I can go into a card shop and choose the card with the prettiest picture on it, or the richest colors, instead of the most impersonal one. I allow her to be who she is and hold no expectations of how she should be for me. In that forgiveness and acceptance, not only am I able to unconditionally love another person, I am also able to forgive myself and love myself more."

Once you understand that you are only jousting at Quixote's windmills, that there are no enemies but yourself, the only choice you have is to accept others for who they are. Once you understand that everything and everyone in your life is a reflection of you, you will also understand that by placing any restrictions or expectations on anyone else you are placing the same restrictions on yourself.

Now may be the time for you to begin the realization that past events no longer have the power to keep your life from being all that it can be. An exciting adventure is ahead of you when you are willing to bring new light upon the shadows of the past, look at your life clearly and honestly, release the weight of past resentments and follow your own path to the future.

Recognition

1. List all of those people for whom you hold any resentment. (Do they know it? Do you think they care?)
2. Sit comfortably in a chair. (Close your eyes after you read the rest of the directions.) Think of a time and a place where you were relaxed and at peace. Now think of a person or situation that you resent. Notice the changes that take place in your body. Mentally scan your body and see where you felt any tension when you moved from peace to resentment.
3. Find harmless, positive ways to release anger. (Yell in the shower or in your closed car. Pound pillows. Allow yourself to vent your anger with that other person, from a stance of "I" as suggested in the previous chapter.)

Response
Answer the Following

1. How long have I held these grudges?
2. Do I truthfully recall the events that I am now holding on to?
3. Who reinforces my grudge? Who agrees with me?
4. Am I getting any value from that reinforcement?
5. What will I gain by punishing another person?
6. Who am I really punishing?
7. How much of my time is spent in plotting revenge?
8. Do I really want to harm another person?

Reinforcement
Repeat the Following

1. Resentment is self-imposed.
2. Revenge has no place in my life.
3. I replace resentment with acceptance.
4. I live from this day forward.
5. It's okay to get angry and release it.
6. Today I am freed from the past.

He done me wrong song

Why let one high C ruin your whole evening?
Beverly Sills

Nobody likes to lose. What do you feel you lost when you dissolved your marriage? Was it material possessions, such as a house, the car, the TV, or was it some false sense of security you felt in having a warm body around to protect you from some unknown enemy? Was it loss of a business that you helped initiate, the investment of time or the humiliation of being rejected?

"I gave him/her the best years of my life!"

"After all I did for him!"

We feel betrayed when we compare the poor return to the heavy investment. We begin to look at how much we gave as opposed to how much we received. We begin to dwell on our personal "soap operas," *The Perils of*

Pauline. "You think you have problems, wait until you hear mine." In conversations with other divorced women, we seem to be competing for the "Martyr of the Year" award.

For several years after Joyce's divorce, whenever people asked her about it, her response would be: "Sure, it cost me a lot of money, but John tried to get me in the only place he knew he could hurt me. He went after custody of *my* children. And after it was over he didn't even see them for almost a year." Notice that Joyce didn't say *our* children. "I told everyone how he had schemed and lied in court to protect his money. He wanted custody, not because he loved his children, but because he was trying to get me to pay him child support." Statements of this kind ran Joyce's life for a long time. What she never considered in those angry days was that maybe he was hurt over the breakup of a long marriage, and was acting not out of any ulterior motives, but out of love. He really wanted to be with his children. Joyce never considered that the lies came as a defensive reaction against the attack he was feeling—the fear of being tossed out of his reasonably safe environment, to be on his own for the first time in many years. "I only considered myself, my feelings and my comfort."

At that time Joyce did not realize how much more difficult it may have been for her husband to make an adjustment from marriage to nonmarriage. Men tell us it is far more scary for them.

The main challenge for ex-husbands is the adjustment of doing those things that were taken for granted in marriage. This is not to say that men demand to be taken care of by their wives, but rather that males are not traditionally trained in these roles. Women, too, play a part in maintaining these roles by assuming that their mate does not want to perform certain tasks. How many of us have ever asked our mates to do the laundry, or the ironing? One friend keeps saying how she hates to do "his socks," yet has never told Joe, nor asked him to do his own socks.

"Maybe, had you asked him, he would have been willing to do his own laundry."

"If I have to ask, it's not worth it."

Role reversals and role sharings are more prevalent today than in the past, but men have had to be taught. If they were not taught by Mom, who wanted to take care of her little boy, then perhaps we need to take responsibility for teaching them, if that is what we want them to do. Men also need to take responsibility for teaching their wives traditional male tasks.

Betty never asked Don to teach her how to change a tire or do other simple tasks because if she knew how to care for herself she couldn't hold Don responsible for things that went wrong, and then resent him for not fixing them correctly. When she became single, she had to do certain things for herself. There was no one to blame. If it wasn't right, Betty knew who was responsible. If we hold our mates accountable for all the good and bad times during our marriage, we will tend to carry that over after our divorce, and lash out to "get even."

WHAT DOESN'T WORK	WHAT WORKS
Trying to Get Even	Get On with Your Life
	Find a Support System

Give Up the Need to Get Even

The following are some notes Sue wrote shortly after her divorce, which point up the anger and resentment she was feeling. Read them and realize that you are not unique, you are not a bad person for thinking negative thoughts, and you can move on.

At your worst moments, for instance when you find your husband hasn't kept the car payments current, or he's had your gas and electricity turned off while you were on vacation, take heart.

About the time you are forced *to sell your house and* uproot *your family, several other things may occur. The collectors of the bills your attorney told you not to pay could be calling and sending you* threatening *letters because* he *did not pay.*

By noticing the words Sue used—"forced," "uproot," "threatening"—you can easily sense the resentment (and the fear) she felt. And that resentment is sometimes reinforced by the necessity of maintaining communication concerning business or personal matters.

Janet answered the phone.

He: Hi, Janet. Listen, things just haven't been going well for me. I've had a lot of extra expenses. There's just no way I can get a check to you this month.

She: You're kidding, Al. Again?

He: Oh, you've got enough. You can handle it.

She: But what am I going to do about the rent?

He: Well, that's your problem.

He hangs up. Janet's resentment comes from a feeling of helplessness and victimization. "He did it to me again." Just hearing the sound of Al's voice on the phone was enough to trigger her rage. And she may feel the same way each time she hears his voice.

Al was being honest with Janet by calling

her and telling her he could not send the money. He may have been rude, but at least he gave her warning. Her anger was less directed at him than at herself, for being so dependent upon Al.

There is nothing wrong with being angry. Venting immediate anger is a healthy and necessary process for Janet. If she's in private, she can yell and call him names, throw pillows or pound her fists into a mattress. She can also choose some vigorous, physical exercise to release the feelings. Once Janet relieves the immediate pressure, she will be able to see more clearly just who she needs to forgive. If she dams up her rage instead, she will only reinforce her role as victim.

If you're feeling like Janet, victimized by your circumstances, you may want to consider some alternatives. Begin by exploring ways in which you can become self-sufficient. Read your local newspapers, ask questions of everyone you know or join a women's networking group. You will find opportunities for added income. Just listen and open your mind to new possibilities.

At a recent business seminar in Atlanta, a self-made multimillionaire described how one woman built a successful business with an initial investment of three dollars. She bought a can of spray paint and a stencil. Going from door to door, she offered to paint address numbers on curbs. Within one month her earnings were in excess of two hundred dollars per day.

By becoming less dependent on others, you can remove that one source of irritation. Had Janet not been so dependent upon her husband's financial support, she would not have become so angry.

Another source of anger comes from feeling personally attacked; we feel as if the other person has done something just to enrage *us*. Instead of expressing our anger honestly, we tend to suppress it.

John brings the kids home two hours late after a weekend and innocently says to his ex-wife, "I hope I didn't create any problems for you. You're not angry, are you?" She may say "No," even though they had previous discussions about being on time. Instead of allowing herself to vent that anger she turns it inward and says, "I'm just disappointed that the kids missed their cousin's birthday party. It's okay." She feels John did it to her intentionally. "He knew we were supposed to be somewhere at noon. I'll fix him!" she thinks. She spends the next few days plotting how to get even. She wonders why she has an unshakable headache.

When we feel attacked, we create in our mind the necessity for counterattack.

Recent articles concerning disease note a

breakdown in our immune system. The body's defense mechanism stops functioning. It no longer is able to fight off the external enemies that ultimately lead to various kind of diseases. Other studies have shown that there is an increased incidence of arthritis and cancer following divorce or bereavement.[1] Could it be that we get so used up in defending what we think is attacking us from the outer world that we don't have the power left to fend off the foreign bodies that invade our inner being?

Maybe the energy would be better used in taking personal responsibility for ourselves. There is no escaping our responsibility for our own behavior. But we can never exercise real control over other people's thinking, so we may as well give up trying.

Express your anger and move on. Recognize that angry feelings are normal and accept them. Also ask yourself what you are really angry about. Is it with yourself for allowing certain things to happen?

We can easily turn our anger into guilt by not being who we think we should be. When we can get to the source of the anger, we can then decide what to do about it.

Dr. Leo Madow explains anger simply as energy. "If people are frustrated, it must come

---

[1] Dr. Theodore Isaac Rubin, op. cit.

out somewhere. We cannot destroy energy, we can only convert it."[2] If you convert your anger into guilt and turn it inward, it will destroy all other aspects of your life. If you try to save up your anger energy and use it later to get even, it will eventually destroy you.

"I don't get mad, I get even!"

Dr. Theodore Rubin says that getting even takes what energy or drive we have within us and places it outside of us, onto the other person, thus giving him power over us.[3]

Betty felt powerless with her husband because he made all the decisions, controlled the finances and dictated her activities. Because she may have felt inferior or threatened by her husband, she (unconsciously, perhaps) gave up her power. Betty could have used that power in all areas of her life but she chose the point of least resistance—her children. Because she felt secure with them, she could feel comfortable expressing her wants and opinions. All that they were, and were to become, was, for the most part, due to her. As an army officer, Don was away for long periods of time. Betty chose the friends her children associated with, the schools they went

[2] Dr. Leo Madow, Institute of the Pennsylvania Hospital, Philadelphia. From an interview in *U.S. News & World Report*, April 26, 1982.

[3] Dr. Theodore Isaac Rubin, op. cit.

to, the clothes they wore. She felt no apprehension in saying "No" to her children, yet she would normally go along with anything Don said.

If you look at each time you are afraid of saying "No" to the people you love, or expressing your true opinion to them, you will probably notice that they seem to have some influence over your life. They may either withdraw their love from you, or their support. In Betty's case, she feared both. "What will happen to me if I say 'No'?"

Other, more subtle uses of power include the helpless act. "I can't lift this." "I can't figure out these tax forms." Look at how powerful these statements are. People most often rush to your rescue. You get exactly what you want without directly asking.

Another manipulative use of power is the threat of impending illness. "Don't do that. You know my heart can't stand the strain." Anytime we may use illness to get what we want or to control others, we are using a tremendous, if destructive and unconscious, power.

You can and do produce enormous effects in your life. The method you use may not always be apparent to you. Notice how you felt when you have used manipulative power to get your way or to get even.

Sue paced the floor. Their appointment was at ten. She had been preparing for this meeting with their attorney since 6 A.M. Joe promised to be on time. Every few minutes Sue glanced at her watch. It was ten forty-five. By eleven she was fuming. At eleven-fifteen the elevator door opened and out stepped a grinning Joe. Sue was thinking, "It's about time you showed," but didn't communicate her rage. If she started an argument now, she might ruin her chances in the meeting. Instead she kept her feelings in, knowing there would be another time for her to get even. At the next meeting, she didn't show up at all. Years later, Sue realized she was not only punishing her ex-husband, but her attorney, his secretary and other clients that could have used the time reserved for her. In addition, what was to be accomplished was delayed two more weeks. Her trying to get even set up a destructive pattern that ultimately resulted in her feeling guilty for what she had done.

Other ways we tend to use our manipulative powers to get even are through voiced or implied threats. "If you don't do this, I won't do that." "Just wait until the next time."

Revenge is self-perpetuating. How much easier and more constructive to use your power honestly and ask for what you really want.

Then you can channel your energy into ways that enhance, instead of detract from, your life.

Get On with Your Life

One thing that comes up during divorce is fear. "What am I going to do now?" Whether you are coming out into the world as a displaced homemaker or a career woman, you may still have the same fears.

Sharon, a young career woman, experienced intense waves of self-doubt in her personal and business life after her divorce. Her fear overshadowed her innate ability to succeed.

"Just before I was divorced, I quit my teaching job and went into insurance sales full time. I had fun! I was the top salesperson in the office. I was winning awards, earning good money and gaining recognition. When I began going through the dissolution of my marriage, when I knew there was not going to be another income, I became terrified. 'What if I can't do it alone? Maybe I was just lucky.' These anxieties paralyzed me into immobility in my business. I went into the office each day with big plans for what I was going to accomplish; yet I could not do anything. I was so controlled by my fear that I could do nothing but exist from day to day. I had to move through that period, gain confidence in myself slowly, daily, until I realized that I was capable and that I could support myself and my son.

"Through my ordeal, Fran and I became close friends. She went through the same turmoil just six months before, so we had much in common. We spent many hours talking about our situations and sharing our feelings. Knowing there was someone else who had felt the way I did was tremendous support for me. In addition to our discussions, Fran would invite me to meetings where I met other people like myself. With Fran close by, the road got easier. My fear subsided and my confidence was subsequently restored."

Don't depend solely on reading, lectures, etc., to get you where you want to go. Beatrice Cole, an octogenarian, was interviewed recently. She said, "...in my career, I never required consciousness raising or analysis to clarify my goals. I had a family to support and money was the main objective...when I go after something I go after it with energy and concentration."[4] Do your reading and studying, but take the next important step, take some positive action. Investigate what you need to do to have what you want and do what it takes to get it. When you're in a rowboat and

---

[4]From an article in *Parade Magazine*, September 1982.

it's sinking, "It's fine to pray to God, but you'd better row to shore."

Find a Support System

One of the things that may stop you from taking direct action is the feeling that you are alone. Realize there are many other women who have gone through similar circumstances. There are organizations such as Parents Without Partners, We Care and various other community groups. You can find them in schools, churches or the private sector. (See Appendix II.) In the beginning it may be difficult to reach out to other people and ask for assistance. But remember you are a valuable person; something you may say within a support group might assist another who is going through the same thing and feeling the same way. When you offer your support to others you're taking the focus off your problems and relieving your own inner pressure.

If you have had experiences with such groups and found one of them unsatisfactory, try another, and another. You will eventually find the group that is right for you.

The only person you can control is you. You can always choose where you want to put your energy: in the past or in the present, negatives or positives. If you are willing to let go of the idea that anyone "did it" to you, and just go forth from today, leaving yesterday behind, your journey will be lighter and easier. You can choose how you want to be, who you want to be with and where you want to go.

Recognition

1. Write down everything you feel "he" has done to you.
2. List all of the responsibilities that were his. (Household chores, finances, repairs, etc.)
3. Write down all the things you feel you did "for him."
4. Write down all the things you feel he did "for you."

Response

1. Am I receiving value from making him wrong? (I'm good; he's bad.)
2. What is my reward in telling my "soap opera" to friends and relatives? (Sympathy, understanding, attention.)
3. Am I willing to look at my life in a new, more positive way?
4. Are all my facts accurate concerning his alleged wrongdoing?

Reinforcement
Repeat the Following

1. I am fully capable of handling my own life.
2. I am honest with myself and with others.
3. No one has done me wrong.
4. I now allow only pleasant thoughts to fill my mind.
5. I see (ex-husband's name) doing the best he knows how to do.

Where did my daddy go?

Bye-Bye Bunting,
Daddy's gone a'hunting...

Nursery Rhyme

Brad, now a teenager, recently told of the feelings he had had as a seven-year-old. "I could sense the turmoil in the house from both my parents. They had tried to cover up their feelings for years, but there was always that unspoken hostility between them that I could intuitively feel."

"Mommy, when is Daddy coming home?" Brad hit the anger switch in his mother. "He's not!" she snapped. "He doesn't want us anymore." He recalled the words his mother had often used. "Now you've got your father mad at me! All our arguments are over you."

We say things to our children when we are hurt that may affect their entire lives. Psychiatrists' offices are filled with people who are still desperately trying to sort out the truth about their parents and what part they, as children, had in the breakup of the marriage. Children usually take on some unwarranted guilt anyway, because they suspect they may have helped to cause the break.

So often we're telling each other how smart and aware our children are, yet we're foolish enough to think they don't know what is going on with their parents in their own home.

Agnes considered herself a good mother who would never intentionally harm her son. But instead of taking the time to sit down and explain how scared she is and how alone she feels, she unthinkingly lashes out. Although she soon forgets what she said, her son does not. He feels responsible. These outbursts are the seeds that can often create a lifelong pattern of self-doubt. "If only I had been better..." "If I had done more to help..." "I must be a bad person or my daddy wouldn't have left me." The child grows up with a feeling that somehow he could have prevented his dad's leaving. He may carry into his adult relationships the fear that those he loves will always leave him.

In addition to feeling responsible, Brad also felt confused. He had considered Dad a hero. His true experience of him was as a loving human—someone he trusted and with whom he was able to share his feelings. They had always had a good time together. Yet, when Brad listened to Mom, he was confused about his own feelings. He can begin to doubt his judgment at a very early age. Should he believe his heart or his mother's spiteful words?

We not only show our resentment in words, but also in the methods we devise to get back at our ex-husbands. Among the methods of retaliation are: not signing important documents; holding on to some of his favorite personal items; showing up late for appointments with him (or not showing up at all); and telling the children about that awful woman with whom "he" lives. If these tactics don't get us what we want, we continue to search for his most vulnerable spot. Sometimes our most valuable weapons are also our most cherished possessions—our children. We sometimes tend to use them as baseball bats.

Agnes and Carl were joint partners in a restaurant business. She wanted it to be part of the property settlement. Carl felt that the restaurant could not succeed under Agnes's management alone, but that he could make it an even bigger success than it was if he maintained ownership. Agnes was bitter and resentful over Carl's affair with the bookkeeper. She was frightened about raising their son by herself, without a solid financial base, which was the restaurant. She also wanted to stay socially involved with her clientele. Agnes felt cornered when the dispute came up in court. After several months of arguments, her chances of winning the restaurant looked slim. Thinking there was no other way, she arranged a meeting with Carl and threatened him: "If you continue to deny me what I want, I'll take Brad to another state where you won't find him."

Carl loved his son deeply. After several loud and heated arguments he knew he had to make the choice. He agreed to give up the restaurant in order to be near Brad. Agnes got what she really wanted, which was revenge.

Agnes recalls that the victory was short-lived. "I felt terrible for using our son that way. I never wanted the burden of running a business, I just wanted to strike back at Carl."

Agnes's guilt came up each time she saw Carl with Brad. She wanted to tell him the truth; instead she perpetuated the lie. When her guilt became too much for her to handle, she sought assistance from her minister. Finding a nonjudgmental person to whom she could tell the truth gave Agnes some comfort. Through her minister's guidance she began to make amends to Carl and their son. When she expressed herself honestly, her resentment subsided. She and Carl worked out an equitable agreement whereby she could still share in the profits of the business, yet would not have to run it.

Most of us are appalled when we hear of someone using extortion as a tactic for gain. We don't want to identify with that but it is still the same thing, according to law. We know that extortionists and hostage takers are ultimately put in jail, but what about our own tactics of "compromise"? When does your method of compromise turn into extortion? Perhaps it is when it comes to "If you don't do what I ask, I won't let you see the children" or "I won't give you back what is rightfully yours." Aside from the legal aspects, what else are you doing to your children?

George was going through negotiations with his estranged wife, Lynn. She informed him regularly that she wanted a certain item of property from the settlement. If he said "No," she kept him from seeing his daughter the next time he was to have her. Lynn is still angry with her in-laws, too, for taking George's side; therefore, she finds ways to keep her daughter from seeing her paternal grandparents as well. What Lynn doesn't realize is that her resentment may have a boomerang effect when her child grows up.

Very often the resenter becomes the resented. If Lynn's daughter follows the usual pattern, she will develop a deep resentment toward her mother. She will not understand why she was kept from enjoying the company of "the other side of the family."

At times the fear of letting the kids be with their dad is valid. If your spouse is using drugs or alcohol, or has a history of violence, you must protect your children. But if your excuse is that he is living with another (particularly a young, pretty) woman, realize that *is* an excuse. Arrangements can be made to protect your children from an environment that goes against your deep, moral convictions. You owe it to yourself and your children to make sure that revenge is not your motive. If you are honest with yourself, you will want to get to the bottom of your real feelings about not allowing "him" to be a dominant factor in your children's lives.

Dorothy and Fred had joint custody of the children, who would spend two weeks with Dad every few months. As their son John got older, Dorothy noticed how much he looked like his father. Every time he spent some time with Fred, he would come home using those little phrases she remembered her ex-husband using. He began emulating Fred's physical movements. When an argument came up between Dorothy and John, she would most often blurt out, "You're just like your father!" As long as she held resentment toward her ex-husband, John was a constant reminder for her. This reminder was one that would keep her mental wounds fresh. Not only was that resentment harming Dorothy, John has also begun to think that if his mom hated his dad, and he was just like Dad, maybe she didn't like him either. Once again resentment had more far-reaching effects than one would think.

Before you take on the guilt of feeling like an ogre, know that awareness is the first step to change. Maybe you have realized you are using the children, and you continue to do so. Most of us do the very best we can at the time we're doing it. In the heat of emotion we often don't see the alternatives. The option is now to calmly tell the truth about what you really want. With that honesty the necessity of holding your children for ransom disappears.

The warranty ran out

'Tis better to have loved and received alimony than never to have loved at all.

Anonymous

"...and the handsome prince took Cinderella astride his beautiful white horse, and swept her away to his castle, where they lived happily ever after."

With all the fairy tales we've read and the love songs we've listened to, it's no wonder we feel betrayed. We expect our reality to be as "they" have told us it should be, and we are shocked when it isn't necessarily so.

If we were raised in a warm, loving environment, with Mom and Dad plus the picket fence, we are programmed to think that is how it should be. "Prince Charming will come and give me a home, nice clothes and fancy cars. We will live together in bliss forever." When a man appears in our lives, and does promise us all those things, our beliefs are reinforced.

If our childhood was one filled with conflict between our parents, or if one or the other married several times, we want our marriage to be different. Somehow we need to succeed where our parents failed. We will go to any lengths to keep a relationship together. Not only do we jump at the chance when someone, almost anyone, promises us eternal love, it becomes almost obsessive with us. We create in our minds a demand that no matter how bad the relationship is, no matter how much it may be destroying us and the other person, we will hang on to it. "After all, I surely don't want to end up like my parents." We look at success not in terms of quality, but in terms of how long we can stay on top. Our lives become endurance contests.

"We insist upon permanence, upon duration and upon continuity."[1]

We all have a tendency to promise to do things forever, even though we have no concept of how long forever can be. "I promise I'll be good, God, if you'll let me out of this one." For how long after you see a terrible accident, or after you get a speeding ticket, do you drive very carefully? When I was

[1] Anne Morrow Lindbergh, as told in a talk by Dr. Leo Buscaglia on public broadcasting, August 1980.

counseling inmates at the county jail, the girls would tell me how it felt to be behind bars. "While I am closed up in here I tell myself I would do anything to get out, and I will never do drugs again because I don't want to be here. When they let me go, I dry-drop[2] the pills before I get to some water."

Relationships can work the same way. In looking at our lives before a significant relationship, we know we want it so much that we will promise just about anything, and mean our promises at the time. Isn't it interesting that later we rarely think of the promises *we* made? Instead, we think only of the promises made to us that have been broken.

What kind of person are you when you first go into a new relationship? "Boy, have you changed!" "You're not the same person I married."

Stewart Emery, well-known speaker and author, uses a phrase. He says some of us are "...walking violations of the truth-in-packaging act."[3] How were you when you first met that significant other? If you were like me, you were all starry-eyed, laughed at all of his jokes and loved his little quirks. "I just love football."

---

[2]A term coined by drug users meaning "taken without any liquid to wash it down."

[3]Stewart Emery is founder of the workshop "Actualizations." His writings include *Actualizations: You Don't Have to Rehearse to Be Yourself* (Garden City, N.Y.: Doubleday, 1978).

"I would enjoy camping out for the weekend anytime." As time went on the truth came out. I really didn't like the outdoors. Camping to me was checking into a motel and having takeout food. I didn't like football, nor did I like that old friend of his. "When a woman marries, she makes a lot of changes: her husband's friends, his manners, his hours."[4]

How long does it take for you to find those little faults with others, the "if onlys"? "If only you would dress better..." "If only you would pick up after yourself..." "If only you would lose some weight..." "If only you were a better lover..." You promised that you would love him just the way he was. Do you condemn yourself for changing your mind? For better or for worse involves both parties, not just him.

For example, most of us promised we would always support him if things went wrong in the business, yet when business goes bad, we tend to blame him.

Laura and Joe had lived from one paycheck to another for most of their ten-year marriage. Joe worked part-time while he was in school. The teaching job waiting for him after graduation didn't pay much more. Laura worked too, but they longed to have those little extra amenities, such as an occasional

---

[4]Anonymous.

movie or a weekend trip. When their first child was on the way, they knew Joe needed to get a higher-paying job. When they discussed how much time the new job would take and how much Joe would have to be out at night, Laura said, "Okay." Five years later, when Joe's responsibilities kept him away from home, Laura was totally unsupportive. "Are you going out again tonight?" "No, I won't entertain your business associates."

In the first blush of romance, even in the first years of a marriage, we think a relationship will continue without change indefinitely. Yet in any healthy relationship, there comes a point when some separate interests develop. It has to happen, otherwise we will suffocate each other.

The changes may occur in careers, leisure activities or other areas of life. Whatever we begin to pursue separately can mean growth in different directions. If you suddenly spend all your time at the gym taking care of your body, you may begin noticing that your partner is out of shape, and that disparity becomes an important issue. If, due to business obligations, your mate spends more hours in bars and uses alcohol or other drugs to relieve his stress, that too may become an issue.

Souls are not saved in pairs. "You're not the person I married" is true on both sides. Look at it realistically and ask yourself if you are the same person you were ten years ago. Do you wear your hair the same length? Have your political viewpoints changed? Are your musical tastes the same? We usually don't notice changes in ourselves, yet when our mate changes we begin to feel out of control. As their position seems to change, we lose our bearings.

Think of it in these terms. You have been traveling a certain route from work to home for many years. You get used to passing by certain stores, neighborhoods on your way. What would happen if the old road suddenly was closed and a freeway was built, circumventing familiar landmarks? You might feel confused, disoriented.

Gloria and her son, Mike, had a tolerable relationship. They each kept busy with their own work and recreation. Conversations together were short. Time together grew shorter as Mike grew older. Gloria sensed they were drifting apart. In school she had been taking a class called "Your Inner Circle of Relationships." She was also influenced by cassette recordings a friend had loaned her. The speakers talked about how important family relationships were. She wanted to form a closer tie with Mike, so she began setting aside more time so they could talk. Having been used to the independence of wandering in and out of the house, no questions asked, Mike was confused at his mother's actions. His assessment was "You used to be a good parent. Now you want to discuss everything."

Understand how your changing may affect other people. If you will put yourself in their place for a moment, you may find how difficult it is for them to accept the change in you. Realize the issue may not be *what* has changed but how they perceive that change. At times they may feel less needed, out of control.

Sue was married to Alan, an aggressive salesman, for twenty-five years. She felt incompetent because Alan habitually told her how dumb she was, that she had no talent, education or formal career. Those opinions had come from the one she thought of as her savior. When they married Sue was drawn to Alan's strength and self-assurance. She didn't realize how overpowering that strength would be, however. Each time she voiced her view about an issue, Alan would tell her, "That's a dumb idea. You don't know anything about it." It was easy for Sue to believe her husband as she reflected on her lack of education. After all, wasn't he supposed to be the head of the household? She trusted his judgment about other things, so why should she not trust him concerning her helplessness? It was not until Sue sought professional advice during the breakup of her marriage that she realized how Alan had manipulated her into believing she was incapable, in order to control her and keep her at home. When she understood this, she began to accept her capabilities.

Why wait until death or divorce to achieve your potential? Why not explore your talents now, before it becomes a matter of survival?

The Cinderella Complex[5] kind of thinking establishes the concept that disaster is imminent. Using your mind to its fullest and developing a fulfilling career direction is sound. But why do it "just in case"—"just in case he dies" or "just in case he divorces you"? Why not do it because it is nurturing to you as an individual and to those you come in contact with, as well as to your relationship with your mate?

Jennifer was married for more than ten years before she went back to school and pursued a career. Earlier in her marriage she felt left out of any kind of intellectual or newsworthy discussions. "I was so into my world of housecleaning and child-rearing that I didn't take the time to read anything that was not pertinent to my little world. I had nothing to talk about at parties, or when we went out to dinner, or even to my husband after a while. I could only spend so much

---

[5] From a book, by the same name, written by Collette Dowling, referring to some of the beliefs women have held about their dependence on men (New York: Pocket Books, 1981).

time discussing plans for the house or what I did that day."

Jennifer thought about a job but didn't want to leave the baby for such a long period each day. Then one day an adult education catalog came in the mail and she knew what she wanted to do. "The class schedule I chose allowed me to pick my own hours and be home most of the time. I was excited about my decision. A whole new world was opened to me. I had new interests. I met people in different occupations and I felt myself emerging."

Jennifer's husband did not share fully in her excitement. He was supportive of her, but in some ways also felt threatened. "Maybe she'll meet another man," he thought. He was no longer the central figure of Jennifer's life, nor could he monopolize the attention at social gatherings. He had trouble dealing with the fear that his wife might be more intelligent than he was.

This kind of emergence is threatening to your mate, because you begin to become more independent. However, it can add a new dimension to the marriage, and if your relationship is healthy, it will bring in new vitality. You will find, because you have outside interests, that you take much of your focus off your mate.

When you are attending a class in the

evening, or visiting at a friend's house, you seldom think of whether or not your partner is home waiting for you. In fact, if you are having a good time, you may wish he weren't.

As each partner becomes a complete person, the relationship is strengthened. You stay with each other out of choice, not out of need. You develop that "declaration of interdependence" that says "I love having you around, but I don't need you with me all the time."

When you open yourself to a variety of interests, you can be more excited about life. You find you feel better than you have ever felt before and feelings are contagious. If I am depressed and not satisfied with my life, I will pass that on to you. On the other hand, my happiness is also contagious. I make sure I feel good about myself first; then I want everyone else to be joyous. I want to give that away, and certainly I can't give what I don't have.

How long does true love last? That's an impossible question. When we are in love, we feel it's forever. But as most of us have found out in the real world—instead of movies, magazines and dime-store novels—the question is not how long love lasts, but what we do with it *while* it lasts.

Although we have little control over duration, we are in charge of the quality of the experience, day by day. Ask yourself what you are willing to do to nurture that love each moment. Love is the seed that requires daily attention and care in order to fully blossom.

When we mentally set up the "love is forever" syndrome, we are totally devastated when it doesn't turn out that way. We can experience a tremendous sense of loss and our first reaction, after the shock, is anger. "That other person did not live up to *my* expectations..."

Those expectations may be the ones he can't keep. "You promised to love me forever." "You said you would always be there." "You told me you would *never* lie to me." Of course you feel angry when he doesn't live up to those promises. But when will you be willing to accept how unrealistic the promises were, instead of letting your anger turn into unhealthy resentment?

Why not look at the gifts you received from your mate? "But I gave it all; there were no gifts for me." Not true. You may not be willing to look for them, but they are there. If you truly want to move past your resentment and anger, you must begin the search. Was there anything he taught you that you wouldn't have learned otherwise? Did you form any long-lasting friendships as a result of your marriage? What about your children? If your mate was abusive or cold, maybe your lesson was to see how warm and loving a person you are in comparison. Realizing who you don't want to be is also a gift.

Maybe the divorce was the greatest gift of all. You now get to experience yourself as a whole person, with abilities and talents you never knew you possessed. Step out of the shadows of your resentment and, instead of being angry over what you think you lost, be grateful for what you have found—yourself.

Recognition

1. List the qualities you have always thought a marriage should have.
2. List any promises "he" made to you but didn't keep.
3. List any promises you have made but didn't keep.
4. Think about Numbers 2 and 3 again.

Response
Answer the Following

1. How long do you think a marriage should last?
2. What is the one promise he didn't keep to you that you particularly resent?
3. What do I want in my life today?
4. What am I willing to do for it?

Reinforcement
Repeat the Following

1. People always tell me the truth.
2. It's okay for me to tell the truth.
3. I can do whatever I like.
4. There is nothing "out there" to stop me from doing anything.

When lovers break up

What shall we call him this time? Whether it's housemate, lover, significant other or posslq,[1] the label is unimportant. The feelings associated with a breakup between two people who have shared intimacy for any length of time can be the same regardless of label.

We will not address the morality of marriage vs. nonmarriage. That's an individual decision. We will, instead, talk about other reasons for choosing one or the other lifestyle. The reasons are numerous. We buy the romantic dream of a never-ending love affair, and some of us have had such negative role models from our parents or other adults, we

[1]U.S. Census term designating "person of the opposite sex sharing living quarters."

swear we will never get married for fear of repeating their tragedies.

Ann and Joe could hardly wait to tell her mother the news. They were to be married this summer. When they walked into the living room they noticed Ann's mom was crying. "What happened?" asked Ann. "It's your dad. He just walked out on me last night," her mother answered. "He wants a divorce." Ann's mom and dad had been married for over thirty years. She could never envision a divorce, but here it was. Now she wondered if she should break the news about her engagement to Joe. How could she now tell her mom that she was about to be married? Moreover, just what does being married mean? Can a thirty year investment end in a husband just picking up and walking out? Fear swept over her. Maybe she was mistaken about the security she thought marriage would bring. Maybe she shouldn't marry Joe after all.

There are those who have been married once or perhaps several times and are afraid of "failing again" or of other people's opinions about multiple marriages. "Did you hear about Sue? She's doing it again! What does this make, her third or fourth? Well, at least she keeps trying, the poor girl."

Sometimes one partner is still married, and for any number of reasons, feels he can't divorce. "My spouse is ill." "I can't afford a divorce right now." "Divorce would put an undue burden on my family." "I can't file yet. My career would suffer too much."

Even if both partners are single and available for marriage, other considerations may crop up. Some women of the 80s fear that getting married would mean giving up their identity. Others tenaciously hang on to their own identity and even retain their maiden name after marriage to signify their independence. Yet there are those women who delight in saying, "I'm Mrs. so-and-so." They feel the label gives them permanence, respectability, belonging and success. They are comfortable in the security of being Mrs. so-an-so and are willing to blend their identity with that of their husband. Still others may think, "I'm willing to live with him as a temporary measure, but I expect it to lead to marriage."

Some live-in relationships begin with the clear understanding that they will eventually become marriages. The live-in arrangement is temporary and will change after certain outside responsibilities are met. The woman acts as if she were a wife in every way. The couple is planning for the future, acquiring material possessions jointly, developing mutual friendships and cultivating their extended families. When this relationship ends, the woman feels she has lost a mate, a tremendous investment of time and emotions, her security and her future status in society.

The age of the partners does not make a difference, nor does the duration of the relationship. Recovery is no quicker for single people who have separated after an affair than it is for couples who have been through a divorce. We want to point out that legal documents are not prerequisites for degree of emotional pain. The disappointment of unrealized expectations or unkept promises, the feelings of loneliness, the anger and the fear are universal after any breakup. We have no way of judging another's discomfort. "My pain is greater than your pain," is not a valid assessment but simply an opinion.

Pam and Al had been living together for just over a year. One evening Al showed up with two burly men. The three of them were carrying a large piano on their backs. "Pam, look what I got for us," said Al. Pam was delighted with Al's thoughtfulness and being able to have friends over for a musical evening. One year later their relationship had become purely platonic. Pam and Al were just sharing the same living quarters. The arrangement was fine for Al, but Pam longed to return to their more intimate connection. When Al left the house to move in with another lady, Pam was furious. She felt used and betrayed. The voice in her head told her, "He just stayed here until he found another place to live. I was only a convenience for him." Discovering some things Al had left at the house, Pam quickly threw them into boxes and deposited them on the porch of his new love. Several weeks later, when Al called and said he was sending movers over to pick up his piano, Pam was astonished. "How dare you? That's my piano. You bought it for me." "Why would I do that? You don't even know how to play," Al replied. Pam retorted angrily, "Well, you're not going to get it!" Two months later they were involved in a lawsuit to decide who really owned the piano.

The issue between Pam and Al was never the piano. Pam had no use for the instrument. However, she could use it as a tool to get back at Al for leaving her. Instead of communicating her hurt honestly and letting go of the past, Pam chose to carry the grudge and allow it to control her life. She spent most of her day either talking to her attorney or complaining to her friends. Pam's life was about a piano she didn't want and a man she couldn't have. Does a grudge weigh as much as a Steinway? Sometimes it weighs more.

Pam had known disappointment before. Her first two marriages had ended in bitter divorces. She thought that living with someone without marriage would be different. Reflecting on the past two years, Pam thought about her life with Al. She cared for him when he was ill, cooked dinners, washed his socks and shared his emotional upsets. She had played the role of a wife. But now, she not only felt the pain of separation, but had no legal rights of community property or alimony. Had they been married, the division of property would have been handled in the dissolution agreement. Pam's only recourse now is a costly lawsuit in which she would have to convince the court that Al gave her the piano as a gift. She has no evidence—only her word against his. Pam's friends and family are unsympathetic as well. "That's what happens when you don't hold out for marriage."

It isn't the form of a relationship but the covert expectations that create the feelings that we have. Do we expect a lover to be different than a husband? Are we living together as a tryout period before marriage?

What is a lover? He is romantic, energetic and always wanting to please. He brings us flowers and other unexpected gifts, sets up candlelight dinners and takes us to picnics in the park. When he's around we feel pampered, lovable and loved.

Joan and Tony dated casually for almost two years. Slowly, their relationship evolved into a deep love for each other. Wanting to be closer and share more, they decided to move in together. They spent weekends bike riding or walking along the beach. Going to the movies reminded them of high-school dates. They laughed and held hands. They made love passionately and frequently.

As the months went by, Joan and Tony got busier with their respective careers. Their work demanded more of their time. Joan had always arranged her schedule to allow her time for exercise and play as well as work. Sometimes she would take the time even if she didn't feel like doing so because she was well aware of the necessity of that balance. She also knew how to separate business from her personal life.

Tony began to work ten to twelve hours a day without allowing himself a break. He stopped exercising, paid little attention to his diet and brought his business problems home with him. While Joan had already shut off from business for the day, looking forward to a peaceful, intimate evening, Tony would walk into the house, give her a quick peck on the cheek, and immediately begin pouring out all the challenges of his day. As his stress mounted each day, he would withdraw further and further. Their minimal conversations narrowed to discussions about Tony's job. The pattern became predictable—come home, talk, lie down on the couch and watch TV, fall asleep. There was no intimate candlelight dinner or spontaneous lovemaking. The romance and laughter had faded away. The day-to-day household chores Joan and Tony had agreed to split were falling more and more upon her shoulders. The thoughts entered her mind, "I feel like a housekeeper with a boarder. I'm not willing to do this anymore. After all, I've already had one husband."

When Tony got home that evening, Joan attacked him verbally. "You haven't been pulling your weight around here. I'm not your housekeeper!" Tony replied, "And I'm not your husband. You sound like a nagging wife." Later that night, unable to sleep, Joan thought about their mutual friends, about Tony's little boy whom she adored, and about all the good times they had shared. In spite of all that, she came to a decision that the relationship was over. "What are we going to do about the furniture we bought? I wonder if I'm going to have to give up the apartment? What'll I tell my friends?" Joan was feeling the same pain and disappointment she had felt at the dissolution of her marriage. Somehow, she had thought that it would be easier to break up with a lover than a husband.

Her disappointment turned to anger. "How could he treat me like this? How could he change so much? What happened to my lover?" Joan's warranty had run out.

Both Pam and Joan are facing some of the challenges they would have had as wives. They have property to redistribute and homes to split up. They must go through the discomfort of telling their friends that the ultimate love affair is over. They are experiencing all the similar emotions—sadness, grief, self-pity and guilt. "What's wrong with me? Why can't I have a lasting relationship?" Statements such as these reflect our self-esteem—or lack of it. Self-esteem is defined as a measure of how we are doing based upon our expectations of ourselves.

Breaking up with a man doesn't mean that you can never have a long-term relationship. It doesn't mean that there is anything wrong with you (or the other person). Nor does it show that you have nothing valuable to contribute to others. Feeling, "I'm worthless because nobody wants me," can take over every other area of our lives. We open ourselves to the possibility of proving our unworthiness with destructive behavior patterns. Our careers may suffer, we may take out our frustrations on our family and friends and blame others for our unhappiness.

We may develop the attitude that, "Men are all alike," and build up defenses that will keep us from entering into any kind of close male-female relationship. Our behavior will serve to defeat the very thing we say we want—a lasting relationship.

The form of a relationship, as discussed

before, has little to do with the results. Our unrealistic expectations set up the cycle of romance to disappointment. We need to allow the other person the luxury of being as human as we are. But if we can't measure up to our own expectations we can't expect anyone else to. We must have compassion for ourselves and build upon our strengths.

Any two people living together create day-to-day challenges. Even if ground rules and roles are clearly defined, situations will always arise that will test your patience and affect the quality of your romance. These things are inevitable and natural. You can either adjust to the realities of life together or stay rigid in your idealism that the other person should be perfect. It's no more realistic to think someone else should be perfect than it is for you to think you have to be. If you hold resentment for how it should be, you will always set yourself up for disappointment.

"Insanity," someone remarked, "is doing something over and over again in the same way and expecting different results." How you deal with what happened in the last relationship and the ones before that will determine the quality of all your connections. Your future happiness depends upon rethinking your ideas about marriage, romance and living arrangements. Do you want a husband or a lover? Do you want to keep your privacy or share your living space with someone else? Would you prefer to maintain exactly the lifestyle you now have or are you willing to make some compromises?

A live-in arrangement is a marriage without a license, subject to all the ups and downs, tears and laughter. Neither one is more secure, more permanent or more impervious to pain. A broken romance is a divorce without a marriage. People hurt, hostilities arise and children can be damaged. Whatever form of love connection you choose, make your choice based upon what you want now, not upon what you think might happen later.

Business as unusual

. . . what is called for is nothing less than all of us reconceptualizing our roles.

John Naisbitt
Megatrends

"Ladies and gentlemen, please put your tray tables back and bring your seats to an upright position. We'll be landing in five minutes." As Beth followed the flight attendant's instructions, she was reflecting on how she felt two years ago, coming back from a vacation, dreading the next morning when she would have to go back into the office with Fred, her ex-husband.

She remembered thinking, "At least when other women divorce their husbands they don't have to see them every day." She had already weighed the possibilities of leaving her job of eleven years, but could see that it would have been financial suicide considering the benefits, possibility of further promotion and the state of the economy. She had formed long-term friendships with people at work, friends with whom she could do all those things that really nurtured her, things in which Fred did not participate. She was involved in planning office parties, leading the charity drives and playing on the bowling team. Her work and related activities were truly an integral part of her life.

As the plane touched down at O'Hare Field, the screeching of the tires jolted her back to the present. Tomorrow morning she would be in the office with Fred, and she felt no dread. Having been willing to reevaluate her situation and change her perception of separation of business and personal life, she could now work comfortably with her ex-husband on a day-to-day basis.

Divorce decrees may include property settlements and custody issues, but seldom define the rules and regulations of working together after the dissolution of marriage.

Former spouses may have worked together for many years, like Beth and Fred, as employees for the same company. Other couples may have served on boards of large corporations that they had created during their marriage. Many times couples who have complementary talents, such as actor/director or architect/interior designer, find it to be to their mutual benefit to continue the business relationship. Perhaps the former mates owned a thriving retail or service establishment. If any of these situations happens to be yours, you may find similar challenges after the divorce concerning your work and would appreciate some suggestions to make the going as easy as possible.

We understand what you may be going through. Attempting to create a harmonious work environment with an ex-husband, in spite of all the hurt and pain divorce sometimes brings, is often difficult. But when you are willing to practice the techniques as set down in this chapter, you will clearly see that your past hurts have nothing to do with your everyday business life. Furthermore, you may be surprised to discover that the new methods of communicating and of perceiving business situations will carry over into every other aspect of your life and make you more personally comfortable as well.

Initially, redefine the purpose of your business and set some new ground rules. "Let's work together for the next year and see how it works." Set new goals for your business. Determine where you want to go and see if you are both still in agreement with those specified goals.

Discuss some new rules for behavior in the office. "Please don't barge into my office without knocking." "Respect my privacy." "Let's not set up meetings without consulting each other first." "Don't make any arbitrary decisions without asking me...and please don't call me at my home unless absolutely necessary."

Set some new agreements concerning financial expenditures. You may have to bring in a third party to mediate some business decisions, to handle the finances, to deal with personnel, etc. This person can also serve as the essential buffer to enable the two of you to maintain a more detached and harmonious relationship, and to aid in reestablishing lines of communication.

Clear communication is the most difficult challenge we have. In business and personal matters, your message may be clear but not your meaning. "The boss wants you to do this right now!" "You better get that contract handled by noon." Your purpose may be only to have a justifiable vehicle to vent your anger. Remember, *it's never what you say, it's how you say it*.

Think of a time you had a message to deliver to someone you were angry with and then think of another time you delivered the same message to a friend.

You and Sally have been close friends since you began working together. Your immediate superior asks you to tell Sally to come into his office. You go over to her desk, smile and calmly say, "Sally, Mr. Smith would like to see you for a moment." Sally thanks you and you go back to your department.

When the story is the same but the person is now your ex-husband, watch the scenario. Mr. Smith has asked you to send Joe into his office. Notice, at first you feel resentful because you are the one that has to go get Joe. That takes you away from your job. Any observer could see the rigidity in your body movements as you walk toward your ex-husband's desk. In clipped tones you say, "The boss wants you in his office, now!" and then you walk away as quickly as possible. You haven't even called Joe by name, nor do you give him any time to let you know he heard what you said.

It's Not What You Say, It's How You Say It!

Just as in the previous example of communication, think of other situations that sometimes come up in any office, regardless of the marital status of the people involved. We all hear stories of salespeople "stealing" clients, handling business unethically, being dishonest or irresponsible. If your ex-husband is involved, know that it is the situation that needs to be handled, not the person. Sometimes we allow our emotions to get in the way of our logical business sense and cloud our decisions. Sit down and ask yourself, "How would I react if Sally did this instead of my ex?" Would I think, "I don't believe that," or "Well, I'm not surprised"? How would you handle the same situation given the two different people involved? Be sure you always maintain your own integrity and professionalism so that you can finish each day feeling good about yourself.

In order to insure the continued success of a business, communication must be not only clear, but honest.

Some of the most cutting remarks are the little "inside jokes." "Do you know where Joe is?" asked Joe's secretary. Sheila answered, "How would I know? I couldn't even keep track of him when we were married." If you have a problem with Joe being irresponsible about telling people in the office where he is, tell Joe. He's the only person who can resolve the issue.

Always Go to the Person Who Can Do Something About the Issue

If your ex-husband has not completed a specified task that was expected of him, such as returning a client's phone call, and your usual pattern is to confront him sarcastically, you can begin now to change that destructive habit.

DESTRUCTIVE: Well, you did it again!

CONSTRUCTIVE: Joe, I just got another call from Mr. Jones. How would you like to handle the situation?

Joe may go into a tirade of excuses—why he is right and Mr. Jones is wrong. Simply listen to what he has to say and ask the question again. "How would you like to handle this now?"

Your attitude is most important. Be sure there is no cutting edge to your question. Recognize your task at hand is to resolve the issue in the most efficient manner, not to make Joe wrong. Finding solutions is what you want to accomplish.

If you feel enraged when Mr. Jones calls and says, "Why haven't my phone calls been returned?" don't storm angrily into your ex-husband's office. Sit for a moment, take a few deep breaths and then write down the message as it was conveyed to you by Mr. Jones.

Your message may read as follows: "Sheila, I'm upset because my calls weren't returned. I needed the information by yesterday and Joe knew that. He promised he would get back to me."

Next, ask yourself why you are really angry. You're probably tired of getting calls, feeling blamed and having someone yell at you for something *he* didn't do. You're angry because your work has been interrupted again. It's fine for you to feel angry, but your priority is success and harmony in your business. As a professional, your function is to impartially communicate the message to the person who can do something about the issue.

Once you've conveyed the message, politely and without sarcasm, ask your ex-husband, "How can I assist you? Is there anything I can do to see that these situations don't arise again?"

You may not get your desired result instantly. He may feel you are putting the blame on him no matter how you approach him. He may say, "Mr. Jones shouldn't concern you. He's *my* client." It is imperative that you maintain your attitude of composure, even if you don't feel like it.

The Longer You Practice, the More Real It Becomes

A passive attitude can be most threatening to an angry or insecure person, but if practiced continually, it is *the most effective method* of creating peace and harmony and the best way to clearly and honestly communicate your desires.

"The force generated by nonviolence is infinitely greater than the force of all the arms invented by man's ingenuity."[1]

---

[1] *The Words of Gandhi*, selected by Richard Attenborough (New York: Newmarket Press, distributed by The Scribner Book Companies, Inc., 1982).

When confronted with an angry outburst or a personal insult say "I'm sorry you feel that way." Don't say anything further, just wait. If the other person continues the insults, continues to be angry and raises his voice, repeat "I'm sorry you feel that way." Don't allow yourself to hear a hidden message; don't confuse business communication with personal attack.

The most effective way of doing business is not to stop what you're doing because of an issue, whether it is right or wrong, but to be willing to take care of it at the moment. Do whatever it takes to resolve the problem, and free yourself for the next project. Being a professional is a learned process. Real or imagined hurts stifle our creativity. What is it costing you in productivity when you are spending so much precious time wondering how you are going to make your ex-husband look wrong or prove yourself right?

Observe when anger taints your voice and you begin hitting below the belt. It's very easy, after having lived with someone, to know where he is most vulnerable. But using these tactics only perpetuates the undercurrent of hostilities.

Your purpose is to deliver *all* communications just as they were given to you—in a businesslike manner. That means even if your ex-husband's new lady friend is returning his call in regards to their dinner date, your task is to deliver the message—do your job in a businesslike manner; pleasantly, clearly and quickly.

Breathe and Move On

Learning to phrase your communication properly may seem strange to you at first; however, it works wonders for everyone involved.

OLD WAY: That cigar really smells terrible. I hate it.

NEW WAY: Bill, when you smoke that cigar in the office, the odor makes it difficult for me to concentrate.

OLD WAY: I hate it when you yell. Can't you ever speak normally?

NEW WAY: Bill, when you raise your voice, I really don't understand what you're saying.

OLD WAY: Will you *please* answer me when I talk to you?

NEW WAY: Bill, when you don't answer me I feel left out and confused.

OLD WAY: Why didn't you give me the message that Apex Company called? You never give me *any* of my messages.

NEW WAY: Bill, Apex Company just called me and said they had given you a message for me. May I have it please?

Another destructive game is to intentionally set up people in order to catch them in a lie. Asking questions to which you already know the answers does not have a place in business. When you have just talked to a client and the client tells you he has spoken to your ex-husband that morning, you may greet Joe with "Have you heard from Apex lately?" You had just called the president of Apex to find out when your company could begin the big project. During the conversation you found out that Apex, one of your largest accounts, was pulling their business and moving it to another company due to the poor service it was getting.

Instead of communicating honestly how embarrassed she felt, her feeling that she didn't know what was going on, she intentionally tried to get Joe to lie. Joe was in a "Catch 22" situation. If Joe said "Yes, they called earlier and canceled the contract," she could have said "Why didn't you tell me before I had to hear about it over the phone?" If he had said "No," she could then call him a liar and say "I just talked to them. You never were very good at telling the truth." What were her real feelings? She was disappointed over not getting the contract, she felt left out because she wasn't told, and she felt embarrassed about her ignorance of the matter. What turned into another angry confrontation could have set the tone for future confidences and success in their business.

CONSTRUCTIVE: Joe, I just talked to Apex and heard we lost the contract. I felt a little uncomfortable when I called them, not knowing the circumstances. I would appreciate it if, in the future, you could let me know in some way what's going on so I won't unknowingly step into something like that again.

The Truth Works!

If you are still emotionally involved with your ex-husband, perhaps you should ask yourself how much the business means to you. Can you handle the pain of seeing someone you love each day, knowing that you cannot be with him on a personal level? Can *he* handle being with you?

When ex-spouses work together, the one who is still most emotionally involved can become paranoid about hearing people talk. Do you think others are talking about you? When you see your ex-husband laughing or engaged in conversation with other people, do you wonder if he is laughing at you? How do you feel when a group of people stops talking as you walk closer to them? How much gossiping are *you* doing with your co-workers? You may find yourself straining your ears to overhear phone conversations, looking in wastebaskets for crumpled-up messages. If that is happening to you, make time after business hours to discuss your feelings with your ex. If he refuses to do this just know that you can't stop people from gossiping. They'll tire of it soon, anyway. Ask yourself why you fear people talking about you. Maybe it's your own insecurity. The less time you spend worrying about what people are saying about how you used to be, the more time you have to maintain your professionalism and reestablish a new businesslike attitude. Your priority is to be successful in your own career, and to do the best possible job you can. Then you will not have time to think about the office gossip.

Hearsay Is Not Fact by Any Means

There may come a time when your new lover shows up to pick you up for a lunch date. You can't go on hiding him forever. You can go through the motions of meeting elsewhere, asking him not to call at the office, but how uncomfortable are you willing to be? On the other hand, flaunting the new relationship in front of your ex-husband or constantly discussing it with co-workers may be destructive. This kind of talk has no place in the business and can do nothing but interfere.

Follow the Golden Rule

Remember the new ground rules for a harmonious business relationship with your ex-husband:

It's not what you say, it's how you say it.

Maintain your own integrity and professionalism.

Always go to the person who can do something about the issue.

Recognize your task at hand is to resolve issues in your business, not to blame others for errors.

Breathe and move on.

The truth works.

Hearsay is not fact.

Follow the golden rule.

Practice these techniques. Continue doing them until they feel natural for you. The longer you practice, the more real they will become. If your discomfort does not ease, if you can't handle doing business together, if it is detracting from your life outside the office, then you may reach the decision to change your employment. Give yourself some time to develop your new attitudes. You'll know when you have to move on to something else. If you have a valuable partnership in business and *you* are willing to do whatever it takes to continue, then your opportunities for ongoing success and harmony are infinite.

Recognition

1. Write down all the ways that you were polite and courteous today to your ex-husband. Write down all the ways he repaid your politeness.
2. Write down the ways in which you supported him in his work today.
3. Write down your "excuses" for any unprofessional behavior—when you let your personal feelings interfere with a business decision. How do you feel about other people who make those types of excuses to you?
4. Think of how you talk to and behave toward coworkers. Think of how you talk to and behave toward your ex-husband.

Response
Answer the Following

1. Was I an active listener today?
2. Was I a true professional today?
3. How much time did I spend gossiping?
4. How much time did I spend arguing over an issue?
5. What did I do today to support my business targets?
6. Did I sulk today or not communicate my real feelings about a business issue?

Reinforcement
Repeat the Following

1. Today is a wonderful day for business.
2. I am a hundred percent on target with my work and goals today.
3. I am confident and professional in every way.

4. I know how to negotiate honestly and without manipulation.
5. Everything I perceive as a loss today may be a gain that I don't yet recognize.

Ex-husbands are people too

Sometimes I've believed as many as six impossible things before breakfast.

Lewis Carroll
Through the Looking Glass

"Many a woman would get a divorce if she could figure out how to do it without making her husband happy."[1] What makes us think men's fears and hurts are any different than ours, or that they're out having a good time while we're home worrying about our future?

We not only tend to think that nobody else is experiencing as much pain as we are but that being depressed about divorce and a changing life-style is a uniquely female characteristic. We have visions of men going to different places each night, enjoying their new-found "singlehood" and, in general, living the good life. When we think of our ex-

[1]Anonymous.

husband, we never see him in a dimly lit kitchen eating his meal alone, or at a laundromat folding socks and underwear.

It sounds so glamorous to us when men go on business trips, or off to the Orient on a ship or camping in the back woods. That fallacy comes from storybook characters and movie heroes, the same places we pick up many of our unrealistic ideas.

If you have ever done much traveling, you know how it can become routine and tiring. Waiting for planes, waiting for luggage, staying in a sterile hotel room and eating restaurant food quickly cause travel to lose its glamour. You long for your own bed, a home-cooked meal and all those familiar sounds that mean you're home.

All the romantic, log-cabin wilderness stories leave out the part about the icy-cold temperatures in the morning, the total isolation in the evening and the long hours of driving to get there and to come back home again.

Often the one who is left behind feels the other person is having more fun. That may come from the belief that being away is always a vacation and being home is just being home.

Since we wanted to tell both sides of the story, and since we can only speak from the feminine experiential side, we have interviewed some ex-husbands.

This is not a definitive or widespread study and does not set out to prove any hypothesis concerning *all* divorced men. We have used a small random sampling of some of the challenges our male counterparts seem to face and attempt to show the commonalities between "us" and "them." What you may get out of this is a willingness to look at the flip side and a realization that there is no "us" and "them."

The men we interviewed ranged in age from twenty-seven to fifty-three. The shortest time any was married was eighteen months, and the longest was thirty-four years.

Question: Are you now communicating with your ex-wife?

The general consensus was that although the partners were communicating, it was usually for one or the other partner to complain about something. Communication is the most important facet of any relationship. If ex-mates cannot do it honestly, chances are that it was no different during the marriage. You can decide to be the model for honesty and open communication with your ex-mate or anyone else you meet, and while it may not result in a change in their behavior, it *will* result in more positive relationships for you in the future.

Question: What surprised you most about your actions and/or feelings after your divorce?

Loneliness, a surprising realization of dependency on their wives and a sense of loss were common answers.

When we are in turmoil over a disintegrating relationship, we think being away from that person will bring us peace. What we forget is all the other feelings of that time. The men interviewed not only experienced loneliness, a longing to have someone around, but also fear and guilt.

"I felt divorce was morally wrong."

"I was afraid I would keep failing in subsequent relationships."

"Because my father had left me, I always felt it was wrong to leave."

"I was afraid of what my friends and family would say."

Joyce can relate to those feelings. "When I ended my long marriage, I experienced all the same feelings of failure and guilt over divorce. I was torn by it as a young child, so I vowed I would not go through it. I did not feel so alienated or alone as the men [we spoke to], because I had my children." Although sometimes we feel we could have more freedom without them, they give us a sense of stability, belonging and companionship. Most men don't have that sense. They usually move into a small apartment where their company is the television set and the only daily communication with their children is by phone or letter.

Unlike Joyce, Betty gave up custody of her children and was horrified when her relationship with them changed. She thought it would remain the same, but when she moved to an apartment, away from the stability of the home in which they were raised, they became more distant.

Question: Were children involved and how have they been affected?

Most of the men described their children as being confused over the divorce. The kids felt torn and sensed they were being used as tools in a power struggle between their mom and dad, the people they loved most in the world. In the beginning, children are more prone to be angry with the one who is no longer in the house. Betty realized her children were having those kinds of feelings. This points up strongly how men may feel about leaving their children. They have to work through the guilt of leaving before they can develop a new context for the relationship. Once they work that through, they can enjoy their time together.

If Dad sees the children only on weekends, he becomes a Superman. Both Dad and the kids are on their very best behavior, and all the attention is directed at each other. Since they have little time, they are totally there for each other.

With the passage of time, the routine of daily living for the divorced father becomes more important than the pain of the divorce.

Question: Do you think men and women face similar challenges after a divorce?

Most of the men answered "No," yet their problems are not different from ours. Society trains us to think that men feel one way and women another. Yet the more we are willing to admit to our fears and anxieties, the more we realize we are very much alike.

Question: Where did you get your role model for marriage?

When we write our fairy tale for marriage we seem to think our husband knows automatically what his role should be.

"I didn't know how to act like a father (or husband). I just figured I would be the kind of father I would have liked when I was a kid."

Men fashion their role as a father/husband after *their* father, as the exact opposite of their father or, in some cases, neither.

"I never had a role model."

"My role models were Rock Hudson movies."

"I took my clues from movies and magazines. They were all wrong!"

We tend to hold resentment toward our ex-husbands because they are not what we expected. The truth is that he didn't know how to respond because nobody ever taught him. How sad premarriage counseling is not required where roles and expectations can be defined before the ceremony. Our whole society seems to be grounded on trying to cure something after it happens instead of taking preventative steps to see that it never occurs.

If you are not willing to accept that your husband always did what he thought best, you may be ready for a process of completion and release. Remember, you are only releasing yourself, no one else.

Allow yourself at least ten minutes in a quiet room alone. Place two chairs facing each other. Sit down in one of them. Visualize your ex-husband, or any other person you may be holding resentment toward, in the chair opposite you. If you have a friend who is willing to sit in the other chair, that will work too. Instruct your friend only to ask you questions, not give you feedback. Tell the other person, aloud, everything you have always wanted to say. Tell him what you expected of him as a husband and father. Let him know what you wish he would have done, or what you wish he would do now. Say it all! Keep talking until you have nothing more to say.

When you have said everything, ask yourself, "Am I talking to him, or to myself?" "Do I feel I gave to the marriage and to the children what I just asked of him?" Finally ask, "Who do I really resent for not being and doing enough?"

The preceding technique can bring you phenomenal peace of mind. We have used it many times, personally and with others. Do not be surprised when the last thing you say to the other person is "I love you." At the bottom line, that is the only thing we ever want to say to each other.

Be gentle with yourself and others. People do the very best they can at the time they are doing it. If your ex-husband could have behaved differently, he would have. If you could have been a more loving/understanding parent than you thought you were, you might have done that, too. Both of you did the best you knew how, at the time.

Give up the suppressed anger and resentment now. Look instead at the gifts your relationship brought you. Be grateful for the times you shared, the mutual friends you met and the children. Let go of the past so you can get on with the present . . . and the future —your future.

Recognition

1. Write down all of the accusations you have made against your ex-husband.
2. Now write down all the ones you know to be true.
3. Notice the difference in the length of the lists.

Response
Answer the Following

1. What do you think he has that you don't have?
2. What could he say or do concerning you that would make you feel better about him now?
3. What is the one thing you would like to agree on with him?
4. Is there one thing you are not telling him the truth about?
5. What do you think would happen if you were totally honest with him now?

Reinforcement
Repeat the Following

1. There is no competition.
2. I tell the truth.
3. My opinions are not necessarily the truth.
4. I want for him what I want for me.

Infidelity

"He had been denying it for weeks, but I knew. I watched them look at each other. I felt a rage inside of me I had never known I could feel. How dare he do that to me. And with my best friend!"

Infidelity is traumatic. It seems to be the crime that is the most difficult to pardon. "He's wrong. Even the Bible says so." We have a right to hold on to our resentment, or so we think. We feel justified in our behavior toward him because we are so well reinforced.

Women experience infidelity as the ultimate rejection. All the explanations and excuses cannot take away the feeling that he chose another.

At first, she feels inadequate. "Maybe I'm

not as pretty as I used to be." She questions her own sexuality. "If my lovemaking were more satisfying to him, would he have gone to someone else?" "If I was a better listener, if only I had given more..."

If feelings of self-doubt appear when another woman is involved, they are very often magnified when the "other woman" turns out to be another man. When a woman finds out her husband is having an affair with a man, she doubts her capabilities as a wife, and also her total existence as a woman.

The social stigma of a homosexual affair at first may appear to be insurmountable. However, the same questions remain. "What can I tell our children?" "What if our friends find out?" "How can I live with this?"

Eileen and Robert sat at the bar in an elegant resort hotel. Robert remarked, "This reminds me of the place I was in with someone I care for a great deal." It was Eileen's first inkling that Robert had been having an affair. His work took him out of town and to late-night meetings. She accepted it as a necessary part of his career. Her whole world seemed to drop out from beneath her. It seemed there was nobody else in the crowded room. She asked him calmly, "What do you mean by that?"

Robert explained how he had been carrying on an affair for the past three years.

Eileen's reaction was swift and sure. "You rotten ————. How could you do this to me after all I've done for you?" She didn't realize just how angry she was until the next day when Robert was suffering from food poisoning and she hoped he would die. Her anger was not only directed at Robert but at herself for not discovering it sooner. In further conversations she found out that Robert had not been seeing another woman after all; he had been seeing another man.

"How could I have been so dumb!" All the signs were there. Late business meetings became more frequent. He always seemed as if he was in a hurry when Eileen tried to engage him in conversation. They hadn't been going out together socially for a long while, neither had they had any sexual relations. "I could have competed with another woman, but how can I compete with a man?"

From that day on, Eileen became self-righteous. "I've always been a good wife and mother, kept a clean house, entertained his business associates." As far as Eileen was concerned, Robert had committed the ultimate crime and needed to be punished. Her punishment of him would have included the other person, but she couldn't get to him.

The first thing Eileen did was tell Robert's parents. They didn't want to believe their son was one of "those," but after confronting

Robert, they knew the truth. Eileen told all her friends. One of her closest friends said, "I've known about Robert all along. I didn't want to tell you." "How dare you keep that from me," Eileen screamed. "And I thought you were my friend!"

Eileen made a quick decision. She told Robert she and the children were leaving and that their relationship was over. Her parting shot was "You can bet this is going to cost you everything you own."

Eileen was furious at Robert for doing something that she considered sordid and abnormal. She was angry with herself for not paying attention to the signs, and she resented her friends for not telling her the truth. Eileen had gone through the first three stages of her trauma. She had felt the anger and self-doubt. She went from blaming him, to blaming herself, to blaming others. Such statements as "They're all wrong...I'm right... I'm a wonderful person" are evidence of the feelings of self-righteousness that accompany the third step. From there she will move on to resentment and, ultimately, should she choose, to forgiveness and acceptance.

Amanda's marriage was shaky from the start. In their circle of friends they were viewed as "the perfect couple." Their parties were outstanding social events. They were seen publicly at all the "right places." But what appeared to be an ideal relationship was only a facade. Amanda and Richard argued constantly over anything. She resented his playing golf every weekend and he resented her spending large sums of money on what he felt were unnecessary items.

Divorce never entered Amanda's mind; she just accepted her marriage as being average.

Although there seems to be little similarity between Amanda's marriage and Eileen's, they both experienced the same emotions when their husband's infidelity surfaced. While Eileen was outraged that her husband was seeing another man, Amanda was just as outraged when she realized her husband had been seeing her closest friend.

The hurt is very real, the anger a necessary release. The behavior patterns you set up afterward are what determines the quality of your life.

Amanda's way was to withdraw. She had no desire to speak to her husband, and wanted the divorce over as quickly as possible. She no longer cared anything about him. Eileen chose to be judge, jury and executioner. Her life was centered around paying Robert back. Whatever devious methods she could find, she used. Eileen described herself at that time as "a two-headed monster." But once she made the decision to mete out the penalties, she took on a tremendous responsibility. Eileen had to spend a great deal of time making sure the sentence was properly carried out.

Amanda hated the "other woman." She felt betrayed by her husband and her friend as well. Had Janet not made herself so available, just as she had done before with other men, Amanda's husband would not have succumbed. Amanda was furious at any woman who could have an affair with a married man. Blame quickly turned to resentment.

Resentment of our mate's infidelity manifests itself in the same way resentment of anything does. But if we still carry with us the idea that infidelity is a crime directed *at* us, it will cloud all our other relationships. The causes of infidelity, in fact, are varied, and often have little to do with the wife.

Dr. Theresa Crenshaw, a nationally renowned sex therapist, says, "Some men are designed in such a way that they don't function sexually with a woman that they love, but can function with someone they don't love."[1]

There are many other reasons for infidelity. Our purpose is to go beyond the "soap operas" of the past and get to the solutions. Infidelity is no better or worse, no different than any other issues we have discussed.

In Amanda's case, infidelity was the excuse, not the cause, of her divorce. After all, she

[1]Dr. Theresa Crenshaw's new book is *Bedside Manners* (New York: McGraw-Hill, 1983).

herself admitted to having an affair prior to his. The underlying factor was his inability to tell the truth throughout their marriage. Even when confronted with clear evidence of his infidelity, her husband continued to deny it.

Whatever reason you used for the dissolution of your marriage may have been only the tip of the iceberg. If you will honestly search you may rediscover issues that were always hidden below the surface. The sole act of infidelity itself rarely destroys a long-term, close relationship between two loving people.

Both Amanda and Eileen had a choice. They could stay stuck in their resentment where much of their lives was devoted to getting even, or they could give up the drama of the past. The decision to choose forgiveness and acceptance over resentment was not made overnight in either case. For one, it took several months; for the other, more than ten years.

You can choose how long you wish to be stifled by your resentments. How long do you want to wait?

The fear of separation

A house is built with solid walls; the nothingness of window and door alone renders it usable.

Lao-tse

People describe it in various terms. "... stranded, scared...," "...a driving within me that hasn't found a direction or purpose...," "...terrifying; a feeling of insufficiency."

Just what is this thing called separation? Is it not being able to be with another person, or is it merely a separation from yourself, from that inner part of you that tells you you're okay? Webster defines "separation" as "an intervening space"; "to separate" as "to make a distinction between"; "separate" as "not shared with another, estranged from a parent body, existing by itself."

If we look at separation as an intervening space, we can see how attached we become to others. We don't want any intervening space between us and our loved ones. Yet our physical world shows us the value and necessity of having spaces. Scientists tell us that creation takes place in the spaces between the atoms, not in the atoms themselves. Have you ever been in a cave looking up? When it is totally enclosed you see nothing. Yet when there is a space between some of the rocks, such as a little tiny crevice above, enough light enters to illuminate every detail inside the cave itself. Separation can allow the best part of anything and anyone to come through to the surface. When you separate cream from milk, the waste sinks and the cream comes to the top. The chaff is separated from the heart of the wheat, leaving the best part.

Then why do we feel so devastated when we think of separation from our loved ones? It starts from our feeling of abandonment by our source of life at birth, our mother. We often carry that feeling into adulthood. "Parents should instill in their child at the earliest possible age that abandonment is an illusion..."[1] Otherwise we grow up thinking we always need another person around to make us complete.

If you continue to look for another person to complete your life, to give you happiness, you are in for a series of disappointments,

---

[1]Dr. Paul Brenner, op. cit.

and you are putting a heavy burden on the other person. If you hold another responsible for your well-being, then you may hold him or her responsible for things when they seem to go wrong as well. In effect, when you tell yourself that you don't have control over circumstances in your life, and only he or she can take care of you, you give up your power to someone else.

Every time you go outside of yourself for your happiness, fulfillment is temporary. There are ever-changing things that come and go as long as you live on this earth. Change puts you in fear of loss; jobs, people, places all seem unstable, impermanent and out of your control. And when you are motivated by fear, love goes out the window. When you are fearful, your relationships are run by jealousies: "If I keep him with me all the time he won't have anyone better to compare me with," and anxiety: "I hope I'm being the person he wants me to be."

Laura, rather shy and insecure, didn't like to go to large parties. As soon as they walked into the house, Roger would leave her sitting in the living room and go mingle with the rest of the guests. She didn't know how to converse with people she didn't know well. Laura also felt the other women at the party were prettier and more outgoing than her. She spent most evenings worrying about what

Roger was doing in the other room, and how soon he would be willing to take her home. He was just being sociable and couldn't understand her fears and jealousies.

It is never the actual loss of anything or anyone that causes the fear or depression, it is only your perception of the loss. Clark Moustakas has written a lot about loneliness and fear of separation. He says that the anxious contemplation of the possible forthcoming separation destroys any possibility of experiencing the actual feeling with acceptance. In *Individuality and Encounter,* he says, "... [anxiety due to the fear of separation or loneliness] is often connected with feelings of rejection, with feelings of guilt for not being who one is and for not actualizing one's potentialities."[2]

Remember the story of the Ugly Duckling? He wandered around for so long feeling that he didn't belong, trying desperately to be accepted by his peers. After a long search he found a group of beautiful creatures swimming in a pond. He felt a lightness of heart. Looking at his reflection in the water, he knew he was not a duck, but a lovely swan.

[2]Clark E. Moustakas, *Individuality and Encounter, A Brief Journey into Loneliness and Sensitivity Groups* (Cambridge, Mass.: Howard A. Doyle, 1968). Other books by Moustakas include *Loneliness* (Englewood Cliffs, N.J.: Prentice-Hall, 1961).

His search was over. He could finally be who he really was.

Dr. Leo Buscaglia says it another way. Some people are oranges and some are bananas. If you're really an orange and your partner loves bananas, you can try to be just that. But you can only become an imitation banana, never a real banana.[3]

Even if you could have changed who you were for your mate, or your friend, or your relatives, you never would have been first-rate. You would have tried to be someone else. So give up the idea that if you could have been better, your past relationships would have been successful, longer-lasting and fulfilling. Instead, keep the idea that you did your very best and so did your "other."

If you are ready and willing to deal with your fear of separation, you can begin to experience the strength and joy of being alone. But the joy may not magically appear overnight. More likely, it is a one-step-at-a-time process. Along the way, most people experience tremendous pain.

Laura describes her struggle, recalling the days shortly after her separation from her husband:

---

[3]Leo Buscaglia, in a talk given at Asilomar, Pacific Grove, California, August 1982.

"The pain connects from my stomach, through my entire chest cavity, up into my head. I breathe faster, tears well up from my very center and trickle slowly down my cheeks. I want to be held, and loved, and not just by anyone, but by someone very special to me. It's not a depression: depression paralyzes me. It's not a frazzled, fix-me-with-booze-or-drugs-or-sex feeling. I know nothing artificial can fix it. I also know no other person can fix it. I have to fix it myself."

We experience loneliness or separation anxiety when we are not in tune with ourselves. We are separated from that part of us that says "You're okay, you're a valuable person."

Your loneliness may be felt in the absence of contact with others, but it is not solely being without company. Laura wanted her husband to be with her almost all the time, yet she felt terrible pangs of loneliness even when they were sitting in the same room. "Knowing that he was really not there with me, that his mind was always somewhere else, gave me an empty feeling."

On the contrary, physical distance does not matter when two people love each other. The discomfort you may feel at first separation fades with time. Remember how close you were to your brother, or your best friend in high school or, in other cases, your children. When you were first separated from them you thought you could not bear the sadness. Look at your level of discomfort now. You may talk to them by phone every other week, or correspond by mail. You somehow feel their presence each time you recall times in the past with them.

If having people around dispels the feeling of being alone, why do we sometimes feel so isolated at huge parties or other crowded places? You can merge into a large group of people at a meeting or a party, so much that, as Rollo May puts it, you give up your individual existence. You merge into the group at the price of losing your identity.[4]

No, loneliness does not depend upon someone else being there. One of the delusions is that by surrounding yourself with people you will feel less alone. The truth is that by looking to others for your completeness, you live life as an "other-directed" person, one whose source of direction comes from the outside.

A typically "other-directed" person keeps asking, "Do you think it's okay for me to ...?" He is constantly seeking advice but seldom following it until it agrees with what he thought he should do all along.

—"I'm having a problem with my boss, what do you think I should do?"

[4]Rollo May, *Man's Search for Himself* (New York: W. W. Norton & Co., Inc., 1953).

—"Why don't you talk with him?"
—"He won't understand. I've tried that before."

The dialogue continues with other alternatives presented until the predetermined answer comes up.

—"Maybe you need to look for another job."
—"Yes, I've been wanting to leave this one for a long time."

What is common to all the other-directed people is that their contemporaries are the source of direction...dependence on it for guidance in life is implanted early...[5]

If you are an "other-directed" person, you use others to confirm your beliefs about yourself. It is then logical to assume that being without others (or a significant other) must produce some great anxiety. This is not to say that you should not have guidance from others that you love and trust; it means only that you do have feelings and intuition—teachings from within—that tell you what to do, and to depend solely on another for your direction in life is to deny your own intelligence and self-worth.

[5]David Riesman, Reuel Denney and Nathan Glazer, *The Lonely Crowd* (New Haven: Yale University Press, 1950).

The more you depend upon others for proof of your worthiness and for confirmation of your mental powers, particularly in making decisions, the more you diminish yourself and your options. That is why looking to others for approval and validation only further estranges you from your own power. When a "special"—validating—relationship becomes so exclusive that you are totally focused on your mate or children, you tend to push others away; therefore, when you want someone else to talk to, you have nobody. Remorse and a sense of isolation can be the result.

Betty felt a real social separation, because she was trapped into her marriage relationship. When everyone she knew was participating in parties or sports, she waited for her husband to come home. When he was traveling, she didn't know how to fill her days. "Of course, I blamed him for not being there, especially when a small emergency would come up. I wasn't used to making decisions without his permission." And there was the waiting. "Maybe he'll be home soon, or in a couple of hours." "I can't go out because the kids might come over for a visit." Betty turned down invitations to be with other people because she was a good wife and mother, waiting day after day. Then if they did not show up in time, Betty could blame them for causing her to miss something. Often it is easier to blame someone than to take responsibility for yourself. "Although consciously I was making someone else wrong, it was really an excuse for me not to get on with my own life, apart from that of my family.

"I continued to alienate myself from the outside world. When my marriage ended I realized that I needed to start making my own decisions, fill up my days on my own and meet new people. I was terrified at first but slowly became more comfortable with myself. I understand now that had I remained in that situation I might have still been walking that same old treadmill of cooking, cleaning and waiting."

You can take personal charge of your life. You can go to school, find support networks that are springing up all over the country, pursue your particular interests and find out what else is going on in the world. It is not an easy task at first, but the rewards are too great to pass up. Once you fill your life with many interests, you can add to any close relationships you have by contributing new ideas, new enthusiasm and new creativity. Once your focus is off the necessity of always having someone close to you, telling you what to do, providing validation, you can allow more freedom for yourself and others.

Do relationships ever really end? Can you

think of anyone you have met prior to now who has not taught you something or changed your life, even minutely? Do you think that because you no longer see someone he is no longer in your mind? Philip Slater, in *The Pursuit of Loneliness,* called this pattern "The Toilet Assumption," the notion that unwanted matter, unwanted difficulties, unwanted complexities and obstacles will disappear if they are removed from our immediate field of vision.[6] You know that is not necessarily true.

Think of a disapproving friend or relative. When you are doing something he wouldn't approve of, you almost feel he is there with you. There is no separation except a physical separation.

Each person you have ever met has somehow played a part in who you are now, and they have left something of themselves with you. It may be a child you co-created, or just a memory of a special time. It could simply be the awareness that you need not go through anything like that again. Begin being grateful for everyone who has contributed something to your life. Learn to appreciate and acknowledge yourself for who you are and not for what someone else wants you to be. And be

[6]Philip Slater, *The Pursuit of Loneliness, American Culture at the Breaking Point* (Boston: Beacon Press, 1970).

that person you are, with as much fervor as you can muster.

If it seems difficult for you to talk to someone else, begin by being honest with yourself. The following exercise has proven beneficial. Stand in front of a mirror. Make eye contact with your image. Take three slow, deep breaths. Tell yourself aloud anything you would be hesitant to tell another person about you. Get out all your feelings of resentment, anger and love. When you've said everything you want to say, make use of some of the reinforcing statements at the back of this chapter.

Find those people in your life with whom you can share your honest feelings. In that giving of yourself, you will discover more of yourself. Begin taking time for solitary activities, such as reading, exercising, listening to music or pursuing that hobby you never had time for in the past. To change a long-term behavior pattern sometimes takes more than a day, but it can happen. You will, in time, feel less separated from the world, from that special person in your life and, more importantly, from you.

Recognition

1. List all of those people in your life you felt abandoned you.
2. List all of those people in your life you feel you have abandoned.
3. Think of a person you haven't seen for several years— someone you love. Create a picture of that person in your mind. Spend a few minutes noticing your feelings, warmth, etc. Now think of someone you resent— someone you haven't seen in a long while. Notice those feelings. Recognize that when someone is in your mind and heart, they can't get any closer.

Response
Answer the Following

1. Who do I think is the cause of my unhappiness?
2. How do I handle my feelings of loneliness?
3. How much time do I spend with people I don't really want to be with?
4. Why do I spend time with them?
5. Why do I think people leave me?

Reinforcement
Repeat the Following

1. There is no separation.
2. Nobody left me.
3. I have never left anyone.
4. The people I love are always with me.
5. Create a positive statement that will make you feel good. Take something you have said to yourself ("I can't do anything right." "I'm not good-looking enough.") and turn it around ("I can..." "I am...").

Holding on vs. letting go

Hatred and aggression arise whenever there is attachment [clinging and grasping], for one mobilizes to defend one's attachments.

Buddha

Particularly in times of stress, self-doubt or sorrow, we tend to reflect on all the good things that happened in our marriage. "If only I had someone to take care of me." We remember all the times our husband was kind and considerate, brought us gifts or was sympathetic when we were sick. If we are invited to a gala social event, we remember the time when we looked forward to going out. "At least with him, I had an escort." Who wants to go to a dance without a man? It was a time when we were with other couples, too. "I don't want to be the single woman [the fifth wheel] with all of the other twosomes I've known for years."

In times of financial strife, we sometimes

wish we had someone else to take care of us. "Why do I have to do this by myself? At least I had financial support then." These are signs of living in the past, and a kind of thinking that sets us up for self-doubt and a reevaluation of our decision to go on to something else in our lives.

The mind plays these kinds of tricks on us, because as soon as we can get far enough from the source of our pain, or what we think that source is, we begin to forget why it was we didn't want to be there. Until a new, painful situation arises our memories stay dimmed.

When Susan's ex-husband is doing everything she requests of him—seeing the children often, sending the support regularly—she feels that it may not have been as bad as she thought. However, when he is being his disagreeable, angry self, it triggers all of the old hostilities.

Whenever we experience any self-doubt about our decision to let someone or something go, we begin to wonder if, in fact, there was not something more there that we simply failed to see. When you hear your mate is happier now than he was with you, do you feel that twinge of "It's not fair that his life is working and mine isn't"? "What does she see in him that I didn't?" Maybe you are not yet reconciled to what happened with your relationship—at some level of your mind it is not really finished.

When you give away a piece of furniture you no longer want, you feel good about it. You have allowed someone else to benefit from it and you've made space in your living room for something new. You know that you have made the right decision to pass it on to someone else because you have totally given that item up. Why then, when you see your ex-husband with another woman, do you not want her to have him? When we doubt ourselves, we wonder if we were sufficient, that maybe it wasn't our ex-husband who was at fault but that we were.

"Someone else is better than I am; I wasn't enough for him; I didn't give him enough of what he needed." It has nothing to do with being "enough." When the relationship is right, there is no need to change anything; when it isn't right, it doesn't matter what you do, there will always be something else wrong.

Another belief we may have is one of lack. Interestingly, when we have good health, satisfying relationships and creature comforts, we never deny another person any of it. We want the best for them and for them to have the experience we're having. We share our happiness with everyone. It's only when we think in terms of scarcity, of our own deprivation, believing there's not enough for us, that we want to deny others their share. We never deny others what we have, but only what we think we *don't* have.

When we turn our thinking around and accept that we have every opportunity to have everything we want, we are released from this kind of envy, resentment or anger. We have the opportunity to build our own love relationships, financial stability or physical health and well-being. We are denied nothing but that which we deny ourselves.

"But I still love him." There is no need to deny that emotion. What you can do is allow it to be okay with you. Accept that you still have feelings for him but don't allow yourself to become so obsessed with them that you do nothing else but think about those feelings. To focus entirely on why you can't have the love you want only intensifies your doubts about your own self-worth. You will use that "held-over" love as an excuse not to move on.

You may want to look at the amount of time you spend involved in feeling that love emotion. Be grateful for what you had with your mate. Watch phrases like "I'll never love anyone else the way I loved John." Know that when you mentally release a person from your past, there is always a replacement. Think of a friend who is deliriously happy with her second husband. You, too, have the ability to love again.

Sometimes, as long as we can say "I still love my ex-husband," it protects us from going into a new love relationship. The very thing we say we want, we keep away by putting up that buffer. "I don't want to be vulnerable again."

Risking again is very difficult and we have the choice of whether or not to open up to love again. If you keep a door closed to shut out the noise from the outside, you don't allow any light or air to come in either. When you choose to block out all bad feelings, you also block out the good ones. The willingness to risk is what makes the difference.

Many times Chris would tell people how much she still loved her ex-husband in order to gain a sympathetic ally. "Hang in there, maybe he'll come back," they would say. "Maybe he'll come to his senses." "Poor you." These were all the things that only made her hold on tighter. Chris was hoping for something unrealistic.

"Only in his absence could I fantasize how good it could be if we were together again. However, when we were together for any length of time, I knew our relationship couldn't be. I knew he was not the man I wanted to be with. Only by recognizing that reality could I begin to release that emotion.

"Had I believed the storybook concept of what love is, I would have stayed under any circumstances. I would have watched him die through his alcoholism, given him a comfortable place to be drunk. I would not only have sold him out, but also myself, as well as my joy and aliveness, in order to be with him. I am grateful that, through professional assistance, I found out how unhealthy that kind of love is. Mine was a love that destroyed, not nurtured. Mine was a love that grew out of need, not choice."

Professional counseling can ease you through the rough spots. Counselors are impartial, caring people who will seldom make decisions for you but act as guides in sorting out your confusion. You may avoid seeking professional assistance because of financial worries; most counselors will establish a comfortable payment system for you. There are some free or low-cost county and city clinics as well. Perhaps your reason for not going is the embarrassment of "I should be able to work out my own problems." If you were being sued for a million dollars, you certainly wouldn't try to defend yourself; you would retain an attorney. Asking assistance does not mean you are a weak person. It means you are willing to bring in a professional who knows how to aid you in dealing with your problems.

The loss of a mate through divorce or death can bring up similar emotions and challenges.

Have you ever known someone who was widowed twenty years ago and still says "He died on me"? The words seem to imply that the other person intentionally left just to cause pain for the survivors. When we hold those kinds of thoughts, we are probably harboring some resentment along with doubts about our own self-worth.

Why is it some people hang on to losses for so long and others don't? Could it be that we handle the experience of loss or death in the same manner we handle other things in our lives? We can choose to get through the emotional turmoil and go on with our lives, or we can keep ourselves stuck in the grief.

Olivia and John had a happy marriage. Their two boys sensed that Mom and Dad were not only marriage partners, but friends. Four years ago, John, a U.S. Navy jet pilot, was killed in a plane crash.

They had just bought a house and were due to move into it within a month. Olivia had a choice; stay in the old place or move. With the assistance of friends, who literally walked her through all the necessary steps, she moved into *their* new home. Having been raised with a strong family foundation, Olivia relied on the loving support of relatives and friends throughout her ordeal. During her first year alone, travel became her escape. In the second year Olivia kept busy with various activities outside the home; she and the children sought counseling.

But throughout this time, when she had company, usually old navy friends, she was still talking as if John was alive and it was *their* house. By the end of the second year, Olivia knew she needed to move. She had to leave the old social circle of officers' wives and navy life. She had to leave the house that *they* bought, and move on to begin her life again. "A physical move got me out of the old community. Moving away from the social environment that was my main emotional support was risky, but essential. It was time for me to grow, outside the confines of my old married life, and redefine the parameters of my new life, my singleness."

There seems to be a time, somewhere between eighteen months and two years after a loss, when a physical move becomes necessary. When the judge notified Vera that she would have to sell her house within two years, in order to pay her husband half the equity, she was furious. But when the time came, just about eighteen months later, she was not only ready to move, but developed an intense feeling of discomfort about being there. At the time she thought the house held too many memories for her—a constant reminder of her unhappy married life. But the reasons you choose do not matter. What matters is that you can either make the decision to keep holding on to the old, or move on to the new.

The challenges posed by death and divorce are indeed similar. Olivia was progressing from the pity of "Why me?" to acceptance. Learning that she could be a whole person without a significant other was one of her more difficult tasks. "John was my best friend. Working for balance without him was most difficult. But I knew it had to come from within."

The sense of anger, "Why did you leave me?" also brings up "I'm not sure I can make it without you." As long as we think we need someone else, we can't create anything on our own. We cannot move to acceptance of the loss and, ultimately, recognition of our own abilities.

Whether you are going through the pain of divorce or death, begin to recognize what you are holding on to. Are you holding on to old friends, an idea that you can never love again or the attention your friends' sympathy gives you?

Olivia got through her pain by giving her time to counsel other widows, sharing some of the steps she took. If you want to stop thinking about your own grief, share yourself with others. In that sharing you see that you are not alone, that you have so much to offer and that there are people out there who love and support you. Olivia's greatest growth came when she began volunteering.

The word "volunteer" makes some of us think of some dirty job that no one else wants. In the army when they ask for volunteers, it is usually for KP duty or cleaning the latrines. In school, volunteering often means to stay after school and lose your recreational time. We grow up with the idea "Don't ever volunteer."

To volunteer is "to offer oneself to any service, of one's own free will." Homes for the elderly, hospitals, your local library or charitable organizations are only a few of the organizations that will welcome you. The key point is not to wait until someone asks. Instead, be willing to find out what you would like to do and reach out to the organization or individual that suits you.

Mrs. M, widowed at age fifty, was full of anger and resentment at her husband's passing. "He went and died on me." "He could at least have had some life insurance to help take care of the bills." "He knew he was sick, why didn't he take better care of himself?" She sought her solace in alcohol. Two years later, she found herself alone, confused and physically spent. She knew she had to do something.

When she developed enough courage to leave the house, she was taken to her first

Alcholics Anonymous meeting. The other participants seemed clean, nicely dressed, cheerful—some of them were laughing. She couldn't laugh. Her face just wouldn't form into a smile, so deep was her misery.

The first active thing Mrs. M did at the meetings was to wash cups, clean ashtrays, straighten chairs. That was the biggest thing she could do. And those small tasks made her feel a part of the group. At first she felt very separate, like a guest. But in cleaning off tables, she felt like a contributing member. That's where her real healing started.

From that small beginning, Mrs. M broadened her volunteering, looking for more ways to expand her life, by sharing herself with others.

A few months later she began to attend a community breakfast that presented motivational speakers. She arrived there before 6 A.M. each week to assist in any way she could, selling tickets, greeting people or counting seats. Mrs. M listened attentively to the speakers, picking up valuable information. She was soon asked to be chairman. As time went on, Mrs. M was instrumental in setting up branches of these clubs across the United States, which, in turn, gave her the opportunity to travel.

You have a clear choice. You can hold on to the past and to the people in your past who are no longer here, or you can get on with your life now. Be reminded of Olivia and Mrs. M and take heart:

> I never doubted I would make it. Getting there was the hard stuff. Some people say time will heal all wounds. This is true, but there is [hard] work we have to do, too.

Olivia was willing to reach out to others and give of herself. It was through her giving that her shift back into the mainstream of life was possible. For Mrs. M, cleaning ashtrays was far from being international director of a service club. Both those first steps were necessary. If you are sad, depressed or confused, find a purpose you can pour your whole being into and you will be given back for more than you could ever imagine.

Recognition

1. List all the qualities you love/loved in your ex-mate.
2. Write down everything you miss about the relationship.
3. Write a short letter to your loved one, telling him what you are feeling right now. (Don't send it.)
4. Write a list of organizations or persons for whom you can volunteer. Your local librarian can assist you.

Response
Answer the Following

1. What is the one thing I got from the relationship that I think I can't have now?
2. What am I waiting for him to do?
3. What am I willing to do in order to get on with my life?
4. What amount of time am I willing to give to volunteering?
5. What is my target? What skills do I need to learn?

Reinforcement
Repeat the Following

1. I willingly release all of those people from my past.
2. I am capable of getting on with my life.
3. I attract those people who assist me in moving on in a positive direction.
4. Volunteering makes me feel good about myself.
5. Nobody did it to me.

Decisions, decisions

Our grand business is not to see what lies dimly at a distance, but to do what lies clearly at hand.
                                                    Thomas Carlyle

It's no wonder we have problems making decisions. Even prior to birth, decisions are made for us by others. In the womb, we are not concerned with choice of meals or temperature. In preadult years, our parents are the ones who make most of the decisions about where we live, when to eat and sleep and how to act. In school, there are teachers and counselors who point us in a particular vocational direction. After graduation, we either enter the job market or get married. If our bosses and spouses do not make decisions for us, at least they play a large part in our decision-making process.

During her marriage, Sue was given a list by her husband each morning headed "Things to Do Today." After fixing breakfast and taking the children to school, she would fill the rest of her day with those tasks that he had set before her.

When the marriage ended many years later, "What shall I do today?" became a paralyzing question. Compare that problem of filling up just one day to the rest of her life. How could she possibly decide on what kind of car to buy or where to find a repairman for the washing machine? "Should I stay in this house or move?" Thinking of decisions in terms of an entire lifetime can be overwhelming. Sue needed first to begin with what she wanted to do each day. Where should *you* begin? You can start from where you are right now.

First, write down everything about which you think you need to make a decision. It took Sue a long time to realize that she did not have to make immediate decisions about the entire rest of her life. First, she compiled a list of all the questions that were swimming about in her head. Then she numbered each one according to priority. "Which ones do I really have to decide now? By what date do the others have to be completed?" That gave her a much clearer picture of what really needed to be decided, and when.

Her list started out with twenty-five challenges, all of which Sue thought needed immediate attention. She wrote each one down, painstakingly prioritized them, then reread them to herself. She began working on the three top-priority items, and somehow the rest of the list was taken care of in the process.

Writing down your problems can work a certain magic for you. You will be able to see the issues more clearly and thus eliminate false problems. When you are looking over your own list, the biggest question to ask yourself about each item is "Do I have to make a decision about this now?" More often than not, the answer will be "No."

Fear is probably the greatest hindrance we have in the decision-making process. We are often afraid of making the wrong decision, as if it were going to be a lifetime choice. Yet what is right today may not be right next week, or next year. So what! The ability to be flexible in your life, to make it okay to change your mind, is a sign of maturity and well-being.

What else are we afraid of? Sometimes we fear the loss of approval from others. "If I sell my house and move away, my family is surely going to be upset. My children won't like changing schools. My friends may say it was the wrong time to sell." "If I decide to date a new man, my kids will resent both of us, my friends will say that he's not good enough for me, that he's too old or too young. Worse than that they may say, 'Why don't you act your age?' If I quit my steady, salaried job to go out on my own, my friends may tell me I'm giving up my security, or I'm not being responsible and 'That's a tough business. Why would you want to do that?'"

Grace feared people would judge her for ending a twenty-year marriage. "Getting a divorce was one of the biggest decisions I ever made," she recalls. "Always having been a junior partner to any major decision, it was very easy not to trust myself this time. I thought maybe I should have given it more time. If only I had more patience, it might have worked.

"I was taking on the entire burden, not only for what was going on in my life, but for what was going on in his, too. I felt other people would judge my decision as wrong. They would question my courage and my integrity and call me selfish. They would think that not only was I leaving my husband, but also that I was deserting *them*. I also felt that I was going against my family's wishes to endure it a little longer. Understand that no one ever voiced any of these opinions. I was only imagining what they thought. I was the one doing the judging."

We always think that others are making judgments about us because we are thinking those things about ourselves. In order to set those confusing judgments aside, we need to come back to the present and look at the situation as it really happened. For Grace, the truth was that it was unbearable to be there any longer. The truth was that she and her husband were damaging one another and no longer had anything in common. The truth was that her decision was right for her.

Trust yourself to do what is right for you and for others who are significant in your life. Remind yourself that you are a capable person and then after you have collected all of the information, you're the one who will ultimately make the decision. Share your dreams only with those who will support you and say to you, "Great! I'll be here if you need me." Most important, stop measuring your worth by what others say and learn to put more trust in your own intuitive feelings.

Lois had reserved a ticket on Flight 182 to San Diego. She was looking forward to getting home to her family after an extended vacation. The morning she was to leave she made a last-minute decision to take a later flight. When she landed at San Diego Airport, she heard the news. Flight 182 had crashed just before landing. Almost 150 people were killed. When asked why she changed her mind about taking the flight, Lois answered, "I don't know. I just had a feeling."

When you make the kind of decision Lois did, there is no way you can logically describe the steps that got you there. Intuition is a momentary insight. Sometimes it hits so quickly, you doubt its validity unless you are used to these feelings. It's those times when you bet the horse according to the racing form, when all along you knew the long shot was going to win...and it does. "I should have paid attention to my hunch."

There is no way business schools can teach a course entitled "Business by Intuition," yet many successful business ventures were made on that principle. Drilling for oil in a certain location may go against all expert opinions, but the gusher that eventually comes in is proof enough that the hunch was right. A developer puts up a small subdivision in the middle of nowhere against the advice of his marketing people, and ten years later thousands of houses and businesses spring up in the area.

Intuition in a business or personal decision may have already altered the course of your life. Think of the times you failed to pay attention to that feeling. "I knew I should have taken Joe up on his offer to sell me that stock," or "I had a feeling before we were married that my husband really didn't want to be married."

When you have spent hours agonizing over a decision, why not follow your own intuitive feelings? It could be the best way to arrive at the answer you need.

Be gentle with yourself. Keep in mind that if what you decide doesn't work, forget it! You'll have many more opportunities concerning that particular matter. You know what you want. Trust your decisions, and go after your dream with vigor.

Don't be crippled by the fear of failure. What if I make this decision and it turns out wrong? The question comes from the ego that says "I'm not enough." It comes also from putting so much emphasis on what you do that you lose sight of who you really are. Trying to be a perfectionist will *always* lead to a feeling of inadequacy. You can never be enough, do enough or get enough approval.

Beverly came from a family of seven children. Her way to feel important was to become a superachiever. She amassed awards and degrees, but couldn't find satisfaction in them. The diplomas, once they were in her hands, became just pieces of paper. Becoming an elected official in her community didn't make her feel sufficient either. In trying to be perfect, she could never measure up to her own expectations. One morning Beverly awoke deeply depressed. "My life is not working. I have all the things I thought would make me feel good—the titles, the respect of the community and the success in my business. Why do I still feel empty?" She made a decision to seek professional counseling, which led her to a search inward. It was through learning to appreciate herself for who she was, without any external labels, that she no longer had a compulsion to be perfect. She realized she had always been enough. As her self-esteem increased, Beverly was more and more content with who she was and what she did. She found that, although she valued the opinion of others, it was how she felt about herself that made the difference.

How do you begin to like yourself more? Simply by doing all of those things that make you feel better about yourself. That may be by taking some extra time in the morning for your grooming. It may mean writing notes to those people in your life you have been thinking of, but with whom you've been out of touch. It can mean doing some nice things for others. Whatever it takes to make you feel better about yourself, then do that thing. Little by little, you *will* love yourself more.

In addition to the emotional part of decision-making, there are some logical steps that have assisted Sue.

For instance, when it comes to making a large purchase or the sale of property, Sue learned not to take only the advice of friends. In the past, she had missed many good opportunities by relying on the advice of someone else who, in well-meaning friendship, did not consider the move good for Sue. Instead she asks the experts, the people who know, and if she is buying something, she asks those who already own the item for an objective opinion. We often make mistakes because we don't have enough information.

"If my decision concerns some kind of a written agreement, I take it to a professional for review." Although expert advice usually costs money, the price is minimal in the long run compared to the difficulties that may arise without it.

"If I am making a career decision, I investigate it carefully, talk to people who are already successful in the field, spend several hours at the local library and check with the community colleges concerning a class on the subject." Many times these adult education courses, which are low-fee or no-fee, can be a good method of exploring the basics of a new career field.

Before you make a major commitment concerning your life, test the water in the way that is least costly to you, in both time and money.

One of the biggest problems about finding new direction in your life is the desire to try so many things at once. To spend your energy on many different things is to sabotage your main target or purpose.

Sue went through a long process of trial and error in order to define her higher pur-

pose in life—and that was to be a healthy,
loving, supportive, financially secure person.
She set only those goals which created movement in that direction. To determine whether
or not her decisions supported her purpose,
Sue needed to ask herself, "Is what I am
about to do going to enhance my purpose in
life, or detract from it?" In order to evaluate
her answers she had to set up some criteria
that were valid in her own situation. Another
way she could ask herself the question is
"How does this lead me toward or hold me
back from the goals I've set?"

In our business, if our answers are not
positive, we don't go ahead with a project.
However, there have been times when we did
anyway. But we suffered the consequences of
roadblocks, disappointments and discourage-
ment.

On one occasion we were asked to promote
a local theater group. The contracts were
signed, yet even after that signing, there was
some resistance from the producer of the
shows. At this time we experienced our first
misgivings about continuing with the project.

Our purpose was to be business consultants
to the producer. But slowly, we allowed ourselves to fall into the promoting of the show.
Clearly out of our niche, we began experiencing some serious setbacks. The press was

lukewarm, articles that were personally delivered to editors were somehow misplaced and didn't appear on time, and we received warnings regarding the producer's integrity. A prior commitment was suddenly remembered by management of the proposed theater, which caused the cancellation of two performances. If we had listened to our intuition at the beginning and honestly asked, "How does this lead us toward or hold us back from the goals we've set?" we would not have continued with the project.

When we were finally willing to stop and assess the results of our several months of promotion, we realized that, because we weren't following our intended purpose, the project was less than successful.

Sometimes we jump into the pursuit of our dream and little diversions come up. A friend recently opened up a business. Her goal was to have her own, successful travel agency where she would have people working for her. She could then "make money while sleeping," a phrase that was part of her purpose.

Less than one month after her office opened, a man for whom she had previously done some public relations work called her and wanted to hire her for an event. It was an attractive, lucrative offer, so she leaped at it. Did this support her own purpose? About one month later, another man offered her an opportunity. This time she was indecisive about it. We talked about her dilemma.

Me: What is your purpose?

Her: To have my own business.

Me: Does doing PR work in another area support your purpose?

Her: No, but why do these opportunities keep coming up?

Have you ever noticed that as soon as you decide to go on a diet you get several dinner invitations? If you make up your mind to stay at home on a particular evening, friends seem to keep calling you asking you to go out somewhere. It's as if the universe is saying, "Are you sure this is what you really want?" These kinds of temptations also offer you the opportunity to stick by your decision or abandon it completely.

If you have set your targets or goals, and you keep having conflicts about whether or not you should do certain things, remember "The way out of conflict is to make a decision."[1] If that man in your life whom you don't want to see anymore continues to call you, you can bet you haven't yet made the definite decision not to see him. If temptation comes up for you repeatedly, you probably haven't yet made a definite decision that you are committed to

[1]Foundation for Inner Peace, *A Course in Miracles* (New York, 1975).

keeping. Never forget that your self-esteem grows when you keep those promises to yourself, when you keep your eye on what you know you wanted.

Your biggest challenge may be in admitting to yourself what it is you really want. Sometimes you believe if you state what you want, it won't happen for you. "Maybe I am not trustworthy enough; maybe I don't have the right knowledge." It is much easier to say "I don't know" than to express your desires and then fail. But the willingness to declare the desires removes the obstacle of indecision. The minute you can say to yourself, "I want *that*," the fun begins.

Once you define your purpose, then set those targets that will lead you there. Find a valid method of attaining your goals, then ask yourself, "What are the necessary steps to get me from where I am to my intended result?"

First, make a list of all of those things you are and are not willing to do to fulfill your purpose. If your goal is to make a million dollars this year, ask yourself if you're willing to move to another part of the world to earn the money. Would you rob a bank? Would you go into a business with unethical people? Just what *are* you willing to do? Next, find out how you can accomplish each point. After fully understanding what you have to do, set a time-frame for yourself that is comfortable for you and suits your life-style. Lastly, remind yourself, on a daily basis, that you can succeed if you consistently pursue your target. *Willingness is the key to getting there.*

Along the way, remember that resentment is one of the most important "cutoff switches" that can stop the flow of clear, logical thinking. Other feelings, such as fear or anxiety, can also block the decision-making process, but these usually come and go. Resentment hangs on like a constant fog, clouding your vision.

Once you remove the barrier of resentment, new avenues will open up for you. Your direction is clear to you and those people come into your life who can assist you in getting where you want to go. It often seems that you accidentally bump into them. Life ceases to be a struggle for you, and almost effortlessly, out of your own clarity and your willingness to say what you want, the right things occur. You don't have to force things to make them happen.

Anne Francis, the actress, tells an interesting story. She was taking private flying lessons in the Los Angeles area. She had been taking lessons from the same instructor for some time. One afternoon her instructor began giving her orders to do those things she knew were contrary to other instructions he had given before. As she followed his directions, the aircraft began to go out of control. It rocked and it looped and it did maneuvers it did not normally do. She was scared! Maybe this flight instructor was crazy and wanted his name in the paper: "Flight instructor crashes over the San Fernando Valley with famous actress." He continued to give her orders.

When she finally panicked and began to scream, the instructor said, "Just let go. Take your feet and hands off the controls." It was then she was sure he was crazed, but she had no choice. She followed his orders.

As soon as Anne let go of the controls, the aircraft righted itself. It flew very smoothly all by itself, with no one at the controls. Her instructor explained that airplanes are designed with a principle called "inherent stability." They are made to fly without anyone touching the controls, once they are airborne.[2]

In discovering your own inherent stability, and knowing you can rely on it, you will stop exerting unnecessary pressure in your life. Give up the idea of trying to control each move in order to get where you are going. Once you have made up your mind about your purpose, make only decisions that will support that purpose, and then trust your decisions. Life will be much easier.

Are you ready to give up the struggle?

---

[2]As told by Anne Francis in a talk for Winner's Circle Breakfast Club, San Diego, California, summer of 1982.

Could it be that you have been pursuing goals that sounded good but belonged to someone else? Is there something you want that you haven't yet had the courage to pursue? Your willingness to act upon the formula set down in this chapter will ease the way.

Recognition

1. List all those things you are concerned about today.
2. Prioritize them as to:
   a) Things to do today.
   b) Things to take care of within the next thirty days.
   c) Things to do within the next year.

Response
Answer the Following

1. What is your greatest fear in making any decision?
2. Has anyone made your decisions for you in the past? Who?
3. Do you trust your own decisions?
4. What do you think will happen if you make a wrong decision about that which you consider most important now?

Reinforcement
Repeat the Following

1. I am trustworthy.
2. It's okay to change my mind.
3. It's okay not to decide everything today.
4. I am capable.
5. I make good decisions.

Just what is a love relationship?

Love is the ultimate expression of the will to live.
Thomas Wolfe

How do we establish rules for relationships? We get our ideas from movies, books and other role models. Being swept up in the fantasy of a daytime soap opera may be therapeutic. But learn to separate your fantasies from your reality. To expect your mate to look and act like a character in a romance novel is to put undue strain on your relationship with him.

As children, the only way we determined how a mother and father, or husband and wife, should act was through our parents. We carefully watched and imitated the behavior we witnessed.

Watch little children playing house or office. If Dad is a businessman, the kids will re-create his departure to the office, complete with attaché case, kiss "good-bye" to Mom and out the door. Playing house involves cooking, while making those little remarks we're used to hearing Mom make while she's in the kitchen. The playhouse dialogue reflects what we were used to hearing in our home environment.

Alice reflects on her childhood. "I remember my own father very well. He was a man's man, loved his children and drinking with the boys. He also loved sports. He became, through the progressive destruction of the disease called alcoholism, more abusive, with dramatic mood swings. Although I swore I would never marry a man that drank or was abusive like my father, I eventually re-created that same scene with my own husband."

Our adult relationships stem from the example we experienced as children. If we don't create our own personal approach to them, we will retain the patterns established for us and subsequently re-create all of our relationships based upon someone else's myth.

With the assistance of a therapist, Alice gained more insight into her habit of blaming others. "I can now accept the behavior patterns I once had and look at them for what they are—conditioned childhood experiences. Once I recognized this, I knew that I was causing my own misery, and that it wasn't someone else. I could then choose to let go of my old, childish ways and create new, adult patterns."

Only through forgiveness and acceptance can movement in a positive direction occur. As long as Alice resented someone else for her plight, there was no way she could escape. You have a choice to spend your time resenting your past, or planning your future. To do both is impossible.

Our early role models dictated how we were to act. But what did we grow up thinking about how the other person should act toward us? The other person should always be there for us "...in sickness and in health." That is simply a re-creation of our thinking that Mother should always be there for us when we are sick, hurt or lonely. We tend to look for that in a mate, too.

We think love means always being in agreement, never having an opposing viewpoint when it comes to large issues. Our society supports this by featuring stories in the media about couples who have been married fifty blissful years. "We've never had an argument in all the years we've been married." There is a saying that if two people always agree, one of them is unnecessary.

We somehow see a lack of agreement as being a personal attack on us, instead of a statement on the issue at hand. Total agreement, all of the time, creates stagnation and ultimately points up that one or both of the parties may be avoiding conflict at any cost.

Low self-esteem sets up the martyr syndrome. "I'll do everything for everyone else. It doesn't matter what I want." "Yes, I love to go out and dance and have a good time. John wants to stay home and watch TV every night, but at least he's a loyal husband." How much of yourself are you willing to give up to a relationship? And how long will you allow yourself to go on being dishonest with yourself about how your life is going? Fear of being honest with the other person also indicates how much self-worth we have. "If he knows what I'm really like, he won't love me anymore." It's more likely that when you open yourself up to another person, he or she will not only appreciate your honesty, but will feel more comfortable in opening themselves up to you.

The alternative to being honest in a relationship is having "hidden agendas"—unexpressed or dishonestly expressed wishes, plans or feelings.

Have those adorable teenage salesmen ever come to your door to get you to vote for them or send them to camp? They begin with "Is your mother home?" (If you're over thirty, the flattery puts you off guard immediately.) Next they relate the sad tale of how worthy they are and how hard they work. "Won't you please show your support by voting for me?" The "hidden agenda" is "I want this lady to buy some magazines."

A typical hidden agenda in a relationship is "Call me whenever you like." Three days later you're pacing by the phone. "Living together is fine. I don't want to get married." Six months later you're saying, "This relationship is going nowhere. When will you be ready to make a *real* commitment?" Don't act as if you will settle for something less than you want. "Love is not looking into each other's eyes, but looking in the same direction."[1] Be willing to begin all relationships based on a mutual, shared direction.

Often friends or family influence our thoughts with what *they* think a love relationship should be. Sometimes we doubt our partner who we thought was wonderful, all because of someone else's well-meaning advice.

Alice was happy until those around her began telling her how it "really" should have been, according to their own belief system.

"Alice," said Sally, "how long have you been seeing Ted?"

"About ten months," Alice replied. She was more content with Ted than with any other man she had known before. He showered her .

[1]Anonymous.

with gifts, took her to romantic places for dinner and treated her family as if it were his own. She would have liked to spend more time with him, but accepted that she couldn't because he was still married. "When is Ted going to get his divorce he's been talking about?" inquired Sally. Alice started to think about what her friend had asked. When Ted would leave her house late at night to go home she would think, "When is he going to get his divorce? I really don't like him leaving in the middle of the night. Maybe this relationship isn't going anywhere." The doubts that Sally planted in Alice's mind began to surface. The more Sally mentioned Ted's marital status, the more it bothered Alice. What she thought was a perfect relationship with Ted began to feel less than perfect. When Alice listened to her friend Sally, she became confused about her own feelings. Had Alice stopped to ask herself "Does Sally have the kind of relationship I want?" she may not have listened at all, but trusted her own feelings. Why not create your own expectations of how a relationship should be, based upon what feels good to you? If your relationships nurture you and feel right, don't question their value because of someone else's opinion.

Amanda's myth was that of the knight in shining armor coming to her rescue, another common fantasy that is particularly reminiscent of the 1950s. In retrospect she only saw the underlying idea that accompanied the fantasy. A knight is strong, loyal and ever the rescuer and guardian of his "lady-in-waiting." She expected her husband to be decisive as well as protective, and when she discovered that his emotional strengths were not super-human, and that she was stronger and more assertive, her fairytale assumptions about him went from Camelot to Humpty-Dumpty.

If you could choose a children's story or fairy tale, which one would best depict your own idea of a perfect love relationship?

There is a big difference between having unrealistic expectations of a mate and having some basic wants. In our attempt to form that perfect, unconditional love relationship, we sometimes keep our true expectations a secret. That sets up the game called "Read my mind." "There are things that I want, but I won't tell you. If you love me, you will just know what they are. Besides, if I have to ask, it's not worth it." Who said so?

When we recognize that we are making subconscious demands as well as obvious ones, and are willing to openly discuss them, we can begin to stop our subtle manipulations. We can determine if both parties are capable of playing their respective part in the chosen fairy tale. If we can begin our relationships based on truths and expressed conditions, we don't end up with the frustration of trying to change the rules in midstream.

Most of us have heard the one sure cure. "Why don't you just talk it over with him? Why not tell him what you want?" We all have tried to pick that "perfect time." Finally, the stage is set and we make the attempt at discussion.

"Joe, I think we really need to talk about this."

"No."

"How about seeing a counselor?"

"No."

"When can we talk?"

"I don't know. Stop nagging me!"

You may have already had an experience like this one. It is much easier to establish your rules in the beginning of a relationship. Closely examine your wants and be honest with yourself. Is the man now in your life capable of giving you what you want or are you setting yourself up for disappointment? Are you telling yourself it will be different later? Don't begin any relationship based upon those three deadly words "aisle . . . altar . . . hymn."

Be willing to look clearly at each new relationship you enter by asking yourself, "Do I want this person as he is now or do I think I will change him later?" If your partner is overweight, does it bother you, or will you allow him the freedom to weigh as much as he likes? Do you approve of his style of dress, manners and the way he talks? Will any of these become issues with you? If the answer is "Yes," you may be setting yourself up for turmoil and frustration. Once you start thinking "I would love you more if only...," realize that whatever the other person changes for you, it will never be enough.

Strong-willed Amanda was able to manipulate some changes in her partner. But then it occurred to her, "Is this person doing it for me? How much of himself is he giving up to do what I ask?" The guilt set in.

"I dated a very loving man for two years. We spent most of every day together, and although we each had our own home, we practically lived together. I felt more love from Jason than anyone else in my life. We were ecstatic for the first year, then suddenly it no longer felt quite right. Jason loved to cook, enjoyed eating his gourmet meals and feeding everyone else as well. That was one of his avenues of giving. I was concerned with my diet. He lived a fairly sedentary life, content with puttering around the house. I ran, played tennis, rode a bike. He liked simple, country living and I was a city girl. After several months he stopped cooking so much, changed his diet, went to a fitness center, bought running shoes and watched his weight.

During one of our discussions in the last month of our relationship, one of my comments was, 'I can't continue to watch you give up so many things that give you pleasure in order to please me.' I didn't feel good about myself for that. I felt that in some way I was taking away from him, not adding to his life."

Completing that relationship and changing its form was one of the more positive things Amanda has done for herself and for everyone else in her life. "We talked about everything and told the truth about how we felt. It was a very emotional scene, full of pain and tears. But Jason and I came out on the other side to love and care for each other. Although we are no longer lovers, in the physical sense, we have something very precious—an honest friendship. When we are together the love we have for each other is apparent to everyone. I was able to complete that relationship with honesty, and it is on that same note I now begin and maintain all my relationships. I am grateful for the gifts that Jason gave me."

What qualities do you want in that one person you would choose to spend your life with? Is he the composite of all the slick magazine ads—the Marlboro Man or the Manhattan shirt model—or the latest detective hero on TV? Does your ideal exist in real life? Your image of the perfect mate may have been greatly influenced by your friends, family and the media. People tend to fantasize about two different types—either those that are the opposite of what they are or those who are the same.

If I am looking for someone who is not like me, or keep finding those people who don't have the same interests, intellectual level or personality traits, I will continually feel disappointed. If I am affectionate and fun-loving, how long will I put up with a cold introvert? Just how long will you put up with those cute, but opposite, tendencies before they begin to frustrate you?

If you keep attracting opposite personalities, perhaps it is because you are trying to find something you think is lacking within yourself. If you don't feel complete within yourself, you may keep looking for someone to complete you. You may feel you are lacking something, so you want someone else to make you feel complete. It's like the puppy chasing his tail, thinking it is something detached from him. He doesn't seem to realize that what he keeps going after is really part of him.

Most people with high self-esteem seem to draw compatible people to them. In considering my own ideal mate, I would like him to be health-conscious, energetic, intelligent and witty. I want him to feel a lot of stability in his life's direction, and be a positive, fun-loving person who knows he is in charge of his own well-being. I want him to know that love is measured by quality, not by time or distance. I also want him to love me enough to allow me the freedom to do whatever it takes for me to be all that I am capable of becoming.

When I put all these ideal qualities together, I come out with a truth that at times startles me. "Hey! I'm looking for another me!" I am comfortable enough with myself to know that I would like to be with someone just like me. I also have a deep understanding of the fact that if I want to receive these things, I need first to give, for it is in giving that the rewards are eventually received.

In choosing that person who will share your life for any length of time, it's important to consider the qualities of compatibility, mutual trust, admiration and respect, along with an acceptance of shortcomings. No one is perfect.

Recontexting relationships begins with honesty. Reveal your expectations, ideals and values to the other person. Be sure any agreements are honestly reciprocal. Commit yourself to expressing fear or love at the time that it comes up, not later when it can be used as a tool. Give the other person exactly what *you* want. Be a role model for others, and make it safe for them to tell you the truth. Listen with compassion. Curtail your impulse to judge right from wrong, and allow them to reach their own conclusions without giving them advice. Above all, keep their confidence.

Compromise is an important part of any relationship. In order to come to an agreement about the entire picture of your relationship, you may have to give up something to get something else. Discover what is most important to you, and practice being flexible about the less crucial issues.

If you are willing to ask for what you want from the onset of the relationship and ascertain whether or not that other person can give it, you are on the right path. You will feel freer and experience more love and joy in *all* your relationships than you have ever before thought possible.

Recognition

1. List all the attributes for your ideal mate. (Physical, mental, financial, etc.)
2. Visualize a perfect evening with your mate.
3. List all of your expectations from a relationship.
4. Remember the source of those expectations. (Where did you get those ideas?)
5. List what you are willing to give to a relationship.
6. Compare the differences in the lists.

Response
Answer the Following

1. Why do you want to have a long-term, intimate relationship?
2. What part of you do you usually hold back in a relationship?
3. How much of yourself are you giving up to the relationships you now have?
4. What do you think would happen if you told your mate and/or your friends the truth about how you feel?
5. Do you really care for the people close to you, or do you want them to change for you?
6. Do you think you can change anyone but yourself?

Reinforcement
Repeat the Following

1. I can only change myself.
2. I want for my mate and my friends what I want for myself.
3. All that I give, I give to myself.
4. I attract only those people to me who are loving, supportive and giving.

What are friends for?

I do not wish to treat friendship daintily, but with roughest courage.

R. W. Emerson
Essays VI

Are you still blaming your ex-husband because you don't have many friends now? Do you feel as if somehow his behavior drove them away? Were the people you associated with during your marriage all his friends?

During our marriage we may have had mutual friends that we entertained, vacationed with and, in general, shared company with. Now after the divorce it appears our friends have chosen up sides. If they agree with our ex-mate, we feel abandoned and even betrayed.

Peggy noticed that her longtime friend Ellen had not called her in some time. During Peggy's marriage, Ellen was a daily caller to chat and share events of the day. They always had a good time together and, being close to the same age, they had much in common.

Peggy recalls that she was concerned about Ellen and decided to call. "I told her that I really missed our talks together and would really love to see her soon." Ellen's reply was one that I hadn't expected. "You know I like you, Peggy, but you're a single woman now, and we just don't seem to share the same interests anymore. Furthermore, you know how my husband feels about me going out with a woman that's unattached." Peggy felt tears welling up in her eyes as she hung up the phone. She immediately remembered her ex-husband and how close he and Ellen's husband were. "Well, there goes another friendship down the drain." The phone call with Ellen was just one of the many changes that had been occurring in her friendships. Even during the breakup she could sense the fear in her friends that maybe this could happen to them, as if divorce was "catching" like the flu.

A once warm friendship with another couple can turn cold when they feel threatened by your new life-style. When, as a married person, you are attentive to your friend's husband, she feels safe. Then, after you become single, you see her suddenly change. "I used to dance with Richard all the time at parties. Why is Dottie so angry with me now?"

Dottie is frightened that she may lose her husband. She now sees a single woman, desperately looking for a man—any man.

Richard is also acting differently. When they both were married, Dottie and Peggy often went out together. Richard was never concerned about where they went or what time they came home. But because he's feeling anxious now, he wants to know where Dottie has been and what she has been doing.

For the third time tonight, Dottie asked Peggy what time it was. "What is your problem?" Peggy asked. "You've been looking at your watch all night." Dottie replied, "I told Richard I would be home by ten. He's been waiting up for me lately."

Peggy could not understand why Richard was so concerned now when he hadn't been before. Dottie explained hesitantly, "I didn't know how to tell you this, Peggy, but now that you are divorced, Richard doesn't want me spending so much time with you. He said that your ex called and told him you had been seeing other men before you were divorced."

On this occasion, Richard was indeed concerned. He couldn't seem to concentrate on the work he had brought home, because his mind kept wandering back to his wife's absence. "Now that Peggy is single she is obviously looking for another man. What if Dottie finds someone else too?"

He is also worried that his wife may be exposed to a different life-style that she might like better than the one she has with him. "What if she leaves me?" Richard is doubting the strength of his relationship with Dottie and feeling very insecure about his marriage.

Both parties in a marriage very often feel threatened by single people. They somehow think that the divorce decree has magically transformed their married friend into a swinging single. Everything they have heard about the singles scene has created their impression of that life-style. They think that singles are interested only in casual relationships and are not discriminating in their choice of partners. The subject has come up many times for Richard and Dottie.

Some common statements in a situation such as theirs are: "We don't have anything in common with Peggy anymore." "She's a single woman now and you know her life is not like ours." "Those people have no stability. Most of them don't hold steady jobs, they hang out in cocktail lounges and they move from place to place and from one relationship to another." "I don't want you being around *those* kinds of people."

Although Dottie does not believe all that her husband says about the single life, she begins to think that maybe some of his misinformation could be true. She's noticed that

Peggy has been calling Richard for advice. What used to sound like a harmless phone call now arouses suspicions in her mind. The warning from Richard about Peggy and the doubts Dottie has create a breach in the relationship between the two women.

Peggy and Dottie have simply chosen two different paths. They no longer have any common social bond to hold their friendship together. While Dottie is still talking about what Richard is doing, or what the children said, Peggy has developed other interests in her life. They have little to talk about to each other, so the friendship begins to fade. Peggy must now cultivate new friends in accordance with her new life-style.

Peggy knows she has to find new friends. However, she feels hurt that she can't keep her old ones as well. She resents Richard and Dottie for thinking she has suddenly changed into a "femme fatale." They had been her dearest friends for so many years, and she expected more trust and loyalty from them. She resented her ex-husband for spreading lies about her. If he told stories to Richard and Dottie, who else did he tell?

Peggy needed to look at the entire picture. Richard and Dottie were not attacking her personally. They were just fearful about their own marriage. In an effort to protect or hide what may have been an unstable relationship, they decided they could not include an unmarried person in their life and lashed out at their friend.

"I would never treat them the way they treated me," she thought. "Well, who needs them? All they wanted to do was tell me how to run my life—and most of their advice was wrong."

Peggy didn't want to admit to herself that she was the one who asked for their advice. During the final stormy years of her marriage when she felt she couldn't communicate with her husband, she relied heavily upon the advice of her friends.

If you are asking your friends what you should do, be certain you really want the answer from them. They may tell you something you don't want to hear. If you are looking solely for agreement, don't ask close friends for advice. Just let them know you want them to listen and be a sounding board. Sometimes sharing your ideas with another person and getting your thoughts out allows you to find your own answers. In the event you do ask for advice and the result turns out wrong for you, remember that you asked. Take some of the responsibility for the outcome. Peggy was not willing to be responsible. Instead she found it easier to justify the end of the friendship by blaming Dottie and Richard for meddling and believing her ex-husband's accusations against her.

Some friendships last a lifetime. They can withstand changes in careers, locations or marital status. Arguments between two friends such as these are put in a place of far less importance than the desire to stay friends. Other friendships seem to come in and out of your life from time to time. You may have to give up being with some people you have loved for many years. The process of letting them go is sometimes painful, but necessary. Choosing friends based on mutual interest, mutual trust and the ability to participate in the same activities without guilt will be an important part of your life's decisions. Keep the friendships that are still comfortable for all of you. Be willing to let go of the ones that are not. In making a wise choice concerning those people with whom you spend your time, you will see just how beautiful true friendships can be.

Sex: give or get

Too much of a good thing can be wonderful.
Mae West

How do your feelings about your own sexuality run your life? What are some of the sex-based decisions you have made? Is sex a natural, pleasant part of your living, or does it cause fear, anxiety and estrangement for you?

We learned as children that a prostitute was a bad woman who sold her body for money. Most of us would be appalled if we were thought to be involved in prostitution, but let's take a look at how society traditionally sets up for just that sort of behavior.

In a recent episode of *Laverne and Shirley*, they had dates with "gentlemen" and were told by a next-door neighbor, "When a man puts a coin into a jukebox, he expects songs to be played." The foursome went to a swanky

French restaurant. Looking at the menu, Shirley realized the price of the dinners. When the waiter took the order, she said, "I'll have the hot cereal of the day," trying to diminish her *obligation* for the evening.

There are two facets of the above story: one male and the other female.

From the Middle Ages, men have always done certain things in hopes of winning their ladies' favors. In modern times, any kind of giving can set up score-keeping. You invite me over for dinner or write me a letter. It's then my turn to reciprocate. Not only does it become a you vs. me match, but the amount of the obligation also becomes an issue. If I buy you a handkerchief for your birthday and you buy me a cashmere sweater for mine, I may feel I owe you something more. Is that how we have set up the man/woman give vs. get syndrome?

"If he thinks he can buy my body with a cup of coffee, he's crazy!"

Just what is your price? Are you holding out for elaborate gifts, extravagant weekends or a long-term relationship ultimately leading to marriage?

Where did we get the idea that we have something so valuable to give and that we are getting nothing in return in the sexual act? We set ourselves up as if our body was so precious a treasure that men would pay any price for it. And men play their role well.

Why can lovemaking leave us feeling so empty? It may be that sex without love is empty. But we think the matter is more complicated. Once again we're dealing with hidden agendas, deceptions and failures to communicate genuine feelings and needs.

We all know about stereotypical singles scenes, where lonely people gather and desperately try to find someone to go home with, ostensibly to have sexual relations. But what are they really looking for? Are they all looking for the same thing or just acting out the part they think others want them to? And what are you giving? If you're giving another person the privilege of enjoying your body, then according to the law of retribution, that's what you're going to get back. Do you really want to be held instead, to have the precious human contact that we all crave? Are you afraid to share that feeling because you think the other guy wants something else? Why not tell him? Hidden agendas are not peculiar only to singles. They also occur with married couples.

Cathy was awarded custody of her two children. Not long after that, Larry informed her that he was going to seek custody. One evening he came over to discuss the issue.

They had dinner. Music was playing softly on the stereo. The house was comfortable and the children were asleep. Cathy's notion was to create a mood that would allow her to talk to him regarding his desire to get the children.

The mood of comfort grew into a mood of romance. It seemed quite natural to retreat to the same bed they shared when they were married.

The next morning Cathy's first thoughts were, "Well, that sure worked out great. He really is being nice about it." Cathy spent the entire morning in an elated mood because she felt that all was right with the divorce and the issue of child custody. She went to work with a general feeling of well-being, more than she had felt in a long time.

Midafternoon, her office door opened and in stepped a county marshal. "Are you Cathy Warwick?" "Yes," she answered in a hesitant voice. Her trembling hand received the subpoena requesting her appearance in court at the custody hearing. "How could he do this to me, after I gave my body to him last night?"

Let's notice how Cathy set herself up. She just assumed that sex would solve her problem. She never revealed her "hidden agenda" to Larry, which was "I give you my body and you give me my children." There was no honest communication between them as to what their lovemaking that night meant. Cathy does not want to take responsibility for initiating the proposed exchange. She outwardly blames Larry; inwardly, she is furious at herself. Now she feels she gave him something he wanted and he didn't return the favor.

Are you using "give to get" sex? If you used sex as a means of barter during your marriage, maybe you're continuing that pattern now. Start exploring your motives when you enter into a sexual relationship. Ask yourself if you are telling the truth about what it is you really want.

Larry was swept up in the mood of the evening. Cathy was being pleasant for the first time in months, allowing him to share some of his feelings and ideas. He felt safe with her. For him, sex had nothing to do with their past or their future. His feelings were honest.

Cathy was still mired in her confused notions about sex, love and with her idea that sex meant love or commitment. Larry's unwillingness to give her what she wanted created some guilt in Cathy's mind. "I slept with a man who doesn't love me. After all, if he loved me he would..." As a little girl she learned—in no uncertain terms—that physical release is not sufficient justification for sex. One must be "in love" to enjoy it.

It's okay if that is your belief. You may set

yourself up for guilt later by assuming that your partner has the same belief system and, therefore, must be in love with you.

"To different minds, the same world is a hell, and a heaven." Sexual relationships can either add or detract from the quality of life. The decision is a very personal one. Whatever your choices, you will probably find that to withhold or use sex as a manipulative vehicle can be a devastating experience. To handle sex instead with the same honesty and integrity you would like from others is to integrate it as a natural part of a balanced life.

The greatest expression of love is to be wholly there with another person. Being wholly there means exposing your thoughts, desires and anxieties with another. That's when sex can become totally fulfilling for you. If you want someone to hold you and nurture you, then you owe him that honesty. If that's really what you want but are unwilling to tell him, and he thinks you want only physical release, then you are involved in rape—carnal knowledge using deception. You are also withholding something valuable from that other person, who may want the same thing that you do but is instead acting out his perceived role.

Once you have been away long enough from the pain of your divorce to begin new relationships you will find that they can be as varied as the people involved. You may choose to date one or several different men for companionship only. You can also choose to have relationships that are purely sexual in nature. That's okay too. Set them up any way you want. Just be willing to be honest about your intentions from the beginning. If you go into a relationship guarded, waiting for the attack, you will find yourself in a very uncomfortable situation. Don't climb into bed with someone because you think it is expected of you. Make a definitive choice to do so or not to do so, and base that choice on your inner feelings. If you have a casual relationship that includes sex, and you don't feel good about yourself the next morning, stop it. Do only that which enhances your own self-worth.

Look closely at how often you use sex to get your way. Is sex a form of control over your partner's behavior, a tool for bartering, an obligation or a joy?

Recognition

1. Recall all the times you felt pressured to have sex.
2. Write some of the beliefs you have about sex.
3. List your excuses for having sex. (He bought me an expensive ring, etc.)
4. List your excuses for not having sex. (He didn't give me...)

Response
Answer the Following

1. Have I ever used my children as weapons to get something I wanted?
2. What price, if any, do I put on my body?
3. How do I feel about that?
4. Do I attach strings to my giving?
5. Do I withhold favors for something I want?
6. Which weapons do I use to get my way?

Reinforcement
Repeat the Following

1. I tell the truth about what I want.
2. It's okay for me to experience pleasure in all aspects of my life.
3. I ask for what I want.
4. I give up all manipulations in my life.

Coda: the gifts

Every man's life is a fairy tale written by God's fingers.
H. C. Andersen

When humankind first appeared on earth it was not as a twentieth-century form. A slow evolutionary process has been taking place since the beginning of time. Everything that has happened to us which has prompted this process in any way has allowed us to be the way we appear to be today.

A Neanderthal being would be out of place in this century. It would be foolish for us to go back through history and pack resentment for every creature that forced us to be more awake, more aware—for every force of nature that encouraged us to seek better forms of shelter or clothing.

Everything in your life that has happened to you thus far has brought you to where you are in this moment. That includes every person you have ever met, every place you have ever visited and every situation you have ever encountered.

Some of the greatest advances in our history came from what seemed to be disasters. Think of how people pull together after earthquakes, floods or other destructive forces of nature. They give each other shelter, food and clothing. They forget their everyday problems and band together as a family for mutual benefit.

Look at some of the miracles of science that have emerged from past wars. Advancement in aviation, communications and medicine are some of the more obvious gifts. We all recognize the tragedy and destructiveness of wars and natural disasters. We cannot change what has happened in the past, but we can begin to look for the gifts in everything that life and death give to us.

Go back to the first time in your life when something occurred that you thought was a real disaster. What did you learn and how did the event affect your life afterward?

Laura felt miserable when her parents were divorced. She cried for days. She pleaded and begged them not to divorce. Laura didn't want to choose between them, and she didn't want to move when the house was sold.

Through therapy Laura learned how much better off the whole family was after the divorce.

"Had they not been divorced, my mother would probably not have given birth to my twin brothers and she may never have sought help for her alcoholism, nor would I have had the pleasure of spending time with my father's new wife. One of my gifts was knowing that my father had someone to love and care for him until the day he died."

Choose to look for the gifts life has to offer you today.

Louise, nineteen years old, married her childhood sweetheart. Frank was the man every young lady dreamed of. His good looks and well-built physique were only part of the package. He was a sweet-talking, fun-loving dreamer who loved to make elaborate plans for the future.

Frank's mother and father were alcoholics, and his family life consisted of the kinds of behavior associated with that disease—mood swings, irresponsibility, dishonesty and instability. Orphaned in his teens, he began living off the streets until at age seventeen he enlisted in the U.S. Army, his first real home in years. Four years later, he married Louise.

Frank always liked to drink and gamble. At first Louise didn't recognize he had a problem.

She would occasionally drink with him, but as time went on, he lied more, drank more heavily and money problems developed.

Household funds disappeared from Louise's purse. Money allocated for their daughter, Amy, was lost. Louise gave birth to another child, a son. A short eight weeks later the little boy died. Frank withdrew and Louise was left to arrange the funeral and other matters. There was, of course, no money. Frank then left for parts unknown.

Louise was left with the bills and the responsibility of caring for a small, asthmatic child. For a time she felt anger and self-pity, trying to find solace in drugs and alcohol. She began associating with a group of drug-oriented people who were also wallowing in anger, resentment and misery. They, too, did not want to face a world that seemed to bring so much pain and disappointment.

Louise became ill. She was tired of the questions swimming inside her head. "Why doesn't Frank get a steady job like other husbands?" "If he would only stop gambling..." "Why isn't he a better father?"

She knew her failing physical health and mental anguish could only lead to the destruction of her life. She felt an obligation to her young child to give her the life she deserved. At the moment Louise realized she had to change her mind or die, she began to view

Frank realistically. She saw that he was just being who he was and that no matter how much Louise wanted to, there was no way she could change him. "You can't force him to be or do what he is not. He's just Frank."

With her anger and resentment fading, Louise now had the energy and will to restructure her life. Her health improved daily and her mind was more at peace.

Louise took every opportunity to educate herself, worked at any job she could find and studied at night, taking Amy along when she could. She took more interest in her appearance. Her tiny apartment was always clean and neat. Those small steps started the process of a new context for Louise's life.

Today Louise has a high-paying management position. She has never tried to poison Amy's mind about her dad. Instead, she has always given permission for Frank to see his daughter. He still has not contributed financial support and continues to drink and gamble. Louise knows, however, that what he does or doesn't do has no bearing on the way she now conducts her life with their happy ten-year-old daughter.

Look for Louise's gifts in this story.

The most obvious gift is Amy, who brightens her life and gives her a sense of pride. Had Frank taken care of everything, Louise may not have sought more education, nor would she hold her present job. Out of her need for survival came her self-worth. Alcohol and drugs are no longer a part of her life.

What about Amy's gifts? The dissolution of the marriage saved her from the pain of growing up with an alcoholic father. She was never involved in hearing the arguments of her parents. She had a chance to live in a loving environment, free from lies and manipulations.

Patricia relates her six-year odyssey.

"At the time of my divorce, I was a forty-six-year-old waitress, working nights in a small dinner house. I was doing the only kind of work I had ever been trained for. I felt threatened by the young, energetic waitresses competing for the best customers. I was also frightened at the prospects of ending up like Rosie, carrying trays at sixty-five. Now that I was unmarried, I wanted to build more financial security, and I knew that now I didn't have to ask anyone's permission to make a change. I was encouraged by watching the television shows depicting women who, in later years, returned to school and began new careers.

"I enrolled in college. The hours I worked allowed me daytime hours for study. Seeing all those healthy young people in class led me to take stock in my physical and mental health. I got braces on my teeth, joined a health spa and changed to a more nutritious diet. I joined Toastmistresses, an organization whereby I could overcome my fear of speaking in front of an audience.

"With my confidence bolstered I was able to move on to a different life—traveling with a nationally known public speaker. I was given the opportunity to see the country, stay in first-class hotels, arrange media interviews and dine at the finest restaurants.

"Two years later, a business proposal came up. A young woman whom I had known for several years asked me to join her in a new venture. She had owned a successful real estate corporation, but wanted to move on to something else. We established our business consulting firm in 1981 and wrote our first two books in 1982. My future is now financially secure, and I am doing exactly what I used to dream about.

"In retrospect I see how intense my desire was to stay married. It was extremely painful for me to let go of that relationship. Yet today I am so very grateful—for the divorce, the new friends I have met along the way, for all that I've learned and have yet to learn. What at first appeared as devastation turned out to be a wondrous beginning for me."[1]

Patricia's story is not unique. She grasped

---

[1]Patricia is Patt Perkins.

the opportunities available to her. You have the same choice now. You can live in the past or plan for your future. Through forgiveness and gratitude you can let go of resentment and make room in your heart for all the love that awaits you.

Once you get into the habit of looking for your gifts, the old way of resenting others becomes a shadow from your distant past. Your life takes on a new meaning and every day is another Thanksgiving. You have taken a giant stride forward and you can never go back, nor will you want to.

When you recognize the gifts, there will be nothing to forgive.

No one else can "do it" to you.

If you think giving up resentment has anything to do with being a nice person, you've missed the point. Go back to square one.

Recognition

1. Lie down in a comfortable position. Close your eyes (after you read the rest of the instructions). Allow your mind to drift back to the beginning of your marriage. Recapture a time when your husband taught you something constructive. Make a mental list of those things you can do now that you couldn't do before you were married.
2. Start a list of things for which you are thankful. Notice how many of these things your husband was instrumental in creating. Add to your list weekly. (Home, children, events, skills, etc.)
3. Include in your list those things you gave him.

Response
Answer the Following

1. What are some of the skills I learned during my marriage?
2. What cultural or recreational activities did he introduce me to?
3. Which people do I have in my life now, as a result of my knowing him?
4. What would be missing from my life had I never known him?
5. What would be missing from his life had he not known me?

Reinforcement
Repeat the Following

1. Today I see the gifts in my life.
2. Today I replace resentment with gratitude.
3. Invent your own statements of gratitude. (I am thankful for . . .)

Divorce Service

Dearly beloved
we are gathered here in the sight of God
and in the face of this company,
to undo the bond
of matrimony
honorably and with dignity to all,
for we are all instituted of
God
whether separate or together,
and we are all one.
——— & ———*, wilt thou regard each other as*
human beings
with your own special needs and wants,
to live apart and let go in peace, harmony and freedom
to find your own fulfillment
in your own ways?
Wilt thou love each other as the parents of your children
and mutually cooperate,
for the sake of all of you,
in sickness and in health
and forsaking all ways that do not obtain the greater
good for each other, for yourselves, and for your children,
so long as you both shall live?

Lee Shapiro, J.D.[1]

---

[1]Lee Shapiro is a nationally known public speaker and author. See Appendix I.

Glossary

ACQUIT   Set free from the charge.

AWARENESS   Alertness in drawing inferences from what one sees or hears or learns.

BELIEF SYSTEM   An organized set of doctrines in which we place our trust and confidence.

CODA   A concluding musical section that is formally distinct from the main structure.

COMMITMENT   A pledge or promise to do something in the future; a state of being obligated.

CONSCIOUS   Aware; noticing with a degree of thorough observation.

ENERGY   The capacity for doing work and overcoming resistance (physics).

EXPECTATION   Something considered due or necessary.

EXPERIENCE   To participate directly (verb). Something personally lived through (noun).

FORGIVE   To cease to feel resentment against. To grant relief from payment.

FORGIVENESS   The act of giving up resentment or claim to requital for (synonym); absolve; acquit.

GRUDGE   A strong, continued feeling of hostility or ill will against someone over a real or fancied grievance.

HIDDEN AGENDA   A list or set of plans that is expected, but not disclosed.

INHERENT STABILITY   The built-in capacity of an object to return to equilibrium.

INTERDEPENDENT   Relying upon one another for support, out of choice and not need.

MARTYR   A person who assumes an attitude of self-sacrifice or suffering in order to arouse feelings of pity or guilt in others.

OLD TAPES   Situations or beliefs from the past that sometimes control the present.

PURPOSE   Something set up as an ultimate end even though it might not ever be attained.

RELATIONSHIP   The quality or state of being connected.

RELEASE   The act of letting loose something caught or held in position.

RESENTMENT   A held-in feeling of bitter hurt or indignation from a sense of being injured or offended.

TARGET   A mark to shoot for.

VISUALIZE   To form a mental image of.

VULNERABLE   Liable to increased penalties but entitled to increased bonuses (Bridge).

WILLING   Ready to respond, choose and act.

The preceding definitions are as used in the book.

Appendix I

Suggested Readings

Bach, Richard. *Illusions: The Adventures of a Reluctant Messiah*. New York: Delacorte Press, 1977.

Bentov, Itzhak. *Stalking the Wild Pendulum: On the Mechanics of Consciousness*. New York: E. P. Dutton, 1977.

Bry, Adelaide. *Visualizations: Directing the Movies of Your Mind*. New York: Harper & Row, 1978.

Capra, Fritjof. *The Tao of Physics*. Boulder, Colo.: Shambhala, 1975.

Emery, Stewart. *Actualizations: You Don't Have to Rehearse to Be Yourself*. Garden City, N.Y.: Doubleday, 1977.

Emerson, Ralph Waldo. *Emerson's Essays*. New York: Thomas Y. Crowell Company, Inc., 1926.

Ferguson, Marilyn. *The Aquarian Conspiracy.* Los Angeles: J. P. Tarcher & Co., 1980.

Foundation for Inner Peace. *A Course in Miracles.* New York: Foundation for Inner Peace, 1975.

Francis, Anne. *Voices from Home.* Millbrae, Ca.: Celestial Arts, 1982.

Frankl, Victor E. *Man's Search for Meaning: An Introduction to Logotherapy.* New York: Simon & Schuster, 1963.

Kubler-Ross, Elisabeth. *On Death and Dying.* New York: Macmillan, 1970.

Moustakas, Clark. *Loneliness and Love,* Englewood Cliffs, N.J.: Prentice-Hall, 1972.

Niendorff, John. *Listen to the Light.* Los Angeles: Science of Mind Publications, 1980.

Shapiro, Lee, J.D. *Dear Dad.* La Jolla: Heart Speak, 1981.

Villoldo, Alberto, and Ken Dychtwald, editors. *Millennium.* Los Angeles: J. P. Tarcher, 1981.

Wilber, Ken. *No Boundary: Eastern and Western Approaches to Personal Growth.* Boulder, Colo.: Shambhala, 1981.

———. *Up from Eden, A Transpersonal View of Human Evolution.* Garden City, N.Y.: Anchor Press/ Doubleday, 1981.

Appendix II

Following is a carefully selected, comprehensive list of national groups, running from purely informational to on-site emergency therapy. Among them you will be able to find assistance for whatever *your* personal challenge may be.

We have also divided them into several different headings, which will make the search easy for you. Read through this section, then look in the alphabetized list for names, addresses and phone numbers. Included with each name is a brief description of objectives and services. Your answers are here. You need only make the call.

ABUSED WOMEN'S AID IN CRISIS
GPO Box 1699
New York, New York 10116
(212) 686-3628

Founded 1975—Offers assistance to abused women and their families. Provides on-site and telephone counseling. Serves as a national clearinghouse to provide information and referrals in answer to inquiries from across the United States.

ALCOHOLICS ANONYMOUS WORLD SERVICES
P.O. Box 459
Grand Central Station
New York, New York 10163
(212) 686-1100

Founded 1935—One million + members. International fellowship of men and women who share the common problem of alcoholism.

AMERICAN ASSOCIATION FOR MARRIAGE AND FAMILY THERAPY
924 W. Ninth
Upland, California 91786

Founded 1942—9,000 + members. Professional society of marriage and family therapists. Provides a nationwide referral service.

BATTERERS ANONYMOUS
P.O. Box 29
Redlands, California 92373
(714) 793-7646

Self-help program designed to rehabilitate men who are abusive toward women. Publications: network newsletter, quarterly; national directory, annually. Also publishes *Mutual Support Counseling for Women Batterers*.

COMMUNITY GUIDANCE SERVICE
140 W. 58th Street
New York, New York 10019
(212) 247-1740

Founded 1953—Service agency providing low-cost personal guidance services at private offices throughout the New York City area.

DISPLACED HOMEMAKERS' NETWORK
755 Eighth Street N.W.
Washington, D.C. 20001
(202) 347-0522

Founded 1978. Acts as a clearing house to provide communications, technical assistance, public information, funding information. Provides referrals, publishes *Network News* bimonthly.

DIVORCE ANONYMOUS
P.O. Box 5313
Chicago, Illinois 60680
(312) 341-9843

Founded 1949—A fellowship of men and women who share experiences and who have banded together for the purpose of helping one another with marriage and divorce problems. Publishes monthly newsletters.

EX-PARTNERS OF SERVICEMEN (WOMEN) FOR EQUALITY
P.O. Box 3269
Falls Church, Virginia 22043
(703) 734-9070

Founded 1980—3,000 + members. Ex-military spouses whose purpose is to alert members of Congress to the need for change in laws concerning military benefits after divorce. Publishes quarterly newsletter.

FAMILIES IN ACTION
3845 N. Druid Hills Road
Decatur, Georgia 30333
(404) 325-5799

Founded 1977—3,000 + members. Parents and other adults concerned about drug abuse by young people. Maintains drug information center. Publications: quarterly newsletter and booklet "How to Form a Families' Action Group in Your Community."

GAMBLERS ANONYMOUS
2703 A W. Eighth Street
Los Angeles, California 90005
(213) 386-8789

Founded 1957—Men and women who have joined together in order to stop gambling and to help other compulsive gamblers do the same.

JOINT CUSTODY ASSOCIATION
10606 Wilkins
Los Angeles, California 90024
(213) 475-5352

Founded 1980—600 + members. Psychologists, physicians, counselors, etc. To disseminate information on joint custody for the children of divorce and to survey court decisions and their consequences. Assists children, parents, attorneys, counselors and jurists with implementation of joint custody practices.

MOTHERS WITHOUT CUSTODY
P.O. Box 76
Sudbury, Massachusetts 01776
(617) 433-9681

Women living separately from one or more of their minor children for any reason, including court decisions, exchange of custody with an ex-spouse, etc.

NARCOTICS ANONYMOUS
P.O. Box 622
Sun Valley, California 91352
(213) 768-6203

Founded 1953—2,000 + members. Holds regular group meetings of men and women who share the problem of drug addiction.

NATIONAL ASSOCIATION OF CHRISTIAN MARRIAGE COUNSELORS
P.O. Box 782
Terrell, Texas 75160
(214) 563-1193

Qualified ministers who are actively engaged in marriage counseling.

NATIONAL ASSOCIATION FOR WIDOWED PEOPLE
P.O. Box 3564
Springfield, Illinois 62708

Founded 1980—1,800 + members. Offers widowed persons and their families a better understanding of the problems in dealing with grief and loneliness.

NATIONAL COMMITTEE FOR PREVENTION OF CHILD ABUSE
332 S. Michigan Avenue, Ste. 1250
Chicago, Illinois 60604
(312) 565-1100

Founded in 1972 to increase public awareness. Chapters throughout the country.

NATIONAL COMMITTEE FOR FAIR DIVORCE AND ALIMONY LAWS
75 Spring Street
New York, New York 10012

Founded 1965—2,000 + members. Individuals interested in having antiquated divorce and alimony laws changed.

NATIONAL SELF-HELP CLEARINGHOUSE
City University of New York
Graduate School and University Center
33 W. 42nd Street
New York, New York 10036
(212) 840-7606

Founded 1976—General clearinghouse of information concerning self-help groups. Provides referral services.

NEUROTICS ANONYMOUS
P.O. Box 4866
Cleveland Park Station
Washington, D.C. 20008
(202) 628-4379

10,000 + individuals who now have or have had an emotional illness. No-charge meetings are held where members hear recovery stories, share their experiences and discuss the recovery program.

ORGANIZATION FOR THE ENFORCEMENT OF CHILD SUPPORT
1216 Glenback Avenue
Pikesville, Maryland 21208
(301) 833-2458

Founded 1979—Persons seeking enforcement of laws pertaining to child support. Works with legislative, judicial and administrative branches of local, state and federal governments to improve the child support enforcement system. Educates legislators, courts and the public on the problems involved in collecting child support, makes people aware of their rights under current child support laws. Conducts workshops, maintains hotlines and referral services. Offers speakers and legislative updates, conducts research and self-help meetings. Maintains library of legislative information and government and university books and booklets. Publishes "The Pied Piper," a bimonthly newsletter; holds monthly meetings and conventions.

ORGANIZATION OF WOMEN FOR LEGAL AWARENESS
179 Lincoln Place
Irvington, New Jersey 07111
(201) 762-5208

Founded 1975—12,500 + members. Encourages women to become aware of and to utilize their legal rights. Maintains rosters of lawyers, accountants, psychologists and other individuals willing to donate time and services, library, speakers' bureau, crisis intervention center, displaced homemakers' center and 24-hour hotline. Compiles statistics, produces articles and publications.

OVEREATERS ANONYMOUS
2190 W. 190th Street
Torrance, California 90504
(213) 320-7941

Founded 1960—Includes 6,000 + local groups of men and women who meet to share their experiences, strength and hope in order to recover from the disease of compulsive overeating.

PARENTS ANONYMOUS
22330 Hawthorne Boulevard, Suite 208
Torrance, California 90505
(213) 371-3501

Founded 1970—10,000 + adults who have abused their children and others interested in child abuse problems. Aim is to rehabilitate child abusers and to insure the physical and emotional well-being of their children. They estimate over 5 million children are affected each year.

PARENTS UNITED
Organization deals with sexual abuse of children. Has 24-hour hotline in 71 cities across the United States. There is no national number. Call information in your city or check your phone book. Provides emergency assistance and support groups.

PARENTS WITHOUT PARTNERS
7910 Woodmont Avenue, Suite 1000
Washington, D.C. 20014

Founded 1957—200,000 + custodial and non-custodial parents who are single by reason of widowhood, divorce, separation or otherwise.

REMARRIED PARENTS, INC.
c/o Temple Beth Shalom
172nd Street and Northern Boulevard
Flushing, New York 11358
(516) 349-8174

Founded 1962—Couples who are remarried and work toward success through weekly therapy groups, etc.

SINGLE DAD'S HOTLINE
P.O. Box 4842
Scottsdale, Arizona 85258
(602) 998-0980

Organization serving divorced, divorcing and remarried fathers concerned with continuing relationships with their children from a previous marriage. Acts as a referral service to more than 200 fathers' rights and divorce reform organizations.

THE COMPASSIONATE FRIENDS
P.O. Box 1347
Oak Brook, Illinois 60521
(312) 323-5010

Founded 1973—Nondenominational, informal, self-help organization open to parents who have experienced the death of a child.

THEOS FOUNDATION
306 Penn Hills Mall
Pittsburgh, Pennsylvania 15235
(412) 243-4299

Founded 1962—Established to aid and assist in the planning and development of spiritual enrichment and educational programs for the widowed. Chapters are church-affiliated and nationwide.

VOLUNTEER—THE NATIONAL CENTER FOR CITIZEN INVOLVEMENT
P.O. Box 4179
Boulder, Colorado 80306
(303) 447-0492

Seeks to encourage more Americans to become volunteers. Acts as a clearinghouse for volunteer programs. Maintains a network of 300 affiliated Voluntary Action Centers.

WOMEN FOR SOBRIETY
P.O. Box 618
Quakerstown, Pennsylvania 18951
(215) 536-8026

Self-help group of women alcoholics.

WOMEN IN TRANSITION
112 S. 16th Street
Philadelphia, Pennsylvania 19102
(215) 387-5556

Founded 1971. Provides services to displaced homemakers, women experiencing marital distress, domestic violence, separation, divorce or widowhood. Operates a telephone hotline for information and referrals.

The preceding list was compiled from the *ENCYCLOPEDIA OF ASSOCIATIONS*, 1983, 17th Edition, *NATIONAL ORGANIZATIONS OF THE UNITED STATES*, Denise S. Akey, Editor, Katherine Gruber and Ce Anne Leonard, Associate Editors. Published through Gale Research Company, Book Tower, Detroit, Michigan 48226.

INFORMATIONAL/REFERRAL

American Association for Marriage and Family Therapy
Community Guidance Service
National Association of Christian Marriage Counselors
National Self-Help Clearinghouse
Volunteer—The National Center for Citizen Involvement

PHYSICAL ABUSE

Abused Women's Aid in Crisis
Batterers Anonymous
Parents Anonymous
Parents United

COMPULSIVE BEHAVIOR DISORDERS

Alcholics Anonymous
Gamblers Anonymous
Narcotics Anonymous
Neurotics Anonymous
Overeaters Anonymous
Parents Anonymous
Parents United

CHILDREN RELATED AGENCIES/ORGANIZATIONS

Familes in Action
Mothers Without Custody
National Committee for Prevention of Child Abuse
Parents Without Partners
Single Dad's Hotline
The Compassionate Friends

GRIEF AND LONELINESS

National Association for Widowed People
The Compassionate Friends
Theos Foundation

GENERAL SUPPORT GROUP (Not included in above list)

Divorce Anonymous

LEGAL AND/OR INFORMATIONAL

Displaced Homemakers' Network
Ex-Partners of Servicemen (Women) for Equality
Joint Custody Association
National Committee for Prevention of Child Abuse
Organization for the Enforcement of Child Support
Organization of Women for Legal Awareness
Women in Transition